Water lillies in bloom on one of Hines Ponds.
Photo: Marion Warren

The Pasadena Peninsula

iii

Map used by permission of Maryland Department of Transportation, State Highway Administration

"The past is only the present become invisible
and mute; . . . we are tomorrow's past."

— Mary Webb, *Precious Bane*

Between Two Rivers

A Panoramic View of the Pasadena Peninsula

by

Isabel Shipley Cunningham

with photography by

Marion Warren
and
Thomas Christopher

1999

PASADENA BUSINESS ASSOCIATION

PBA Acknowledgements

The Pasadena Business Association Book Committee would like to say a special thank you to:

Isabel Shipley Cunningham for all the research, writing, teaching, suggestions and the placement of the photographs. Without Isabel, we would have never been able to publish this book.

Marion Warren for copying all the precious original old photographs that were found, restoring and/or touching up some very critical photos and newspaper articles, and for taking very beautiful photos of Pasadena.

Thomas Christopher (Chris) of Blue Moon Aerial Photography for taking pictures of all our sponsors, dozens of community signs and any other picture that we asked him to take.

Michelle Lohin, our intern, for logging over 100 hours looking for existing Pasadena photos in the many photo archives here in Maryland, finding some really significant photos, and carefully picking up and shuttling over 200 photographs to Marion for copying.

Anne Arundel County Trust for Preservation, Inc., and Will Mumford, Trust Chairman, for giving the PBA a $1,000 grant to hire an intern, and for believing in this project and cheering us on.

Sharon Mager for working on the publicity for this book and helping us to get a front page article in the *Gazette* in November 1998.

. . . and last but most importantly, all the **community and business members** who gave of their time for interviews, searched for photos, referred us to the right people and places and supported us as sponsors and patrons and with advice and encouragement.

About the Photographers

Marion Warren: Marion Warren, a native of Missouri, has lived in Annapolis since 1947 and has been the official photographer for Historic Annapolis since its founding in 1952. His published work includes four books of historical photographs, in addition to collections of his own photos. He has taught photography at community colleges and at the University of Maryland and has lectured throughout the state and on Maryland Public Television. MPT's documentary on his career won an Emmy award in 1997. The Maryland State Archives holds a permanent collection of the work of a man who is called Maryland's photographer laureate.

Thomas Christopher, Blue Moon Aerial Photography: Thomas Christopher (Chris), a Viet Nam veteran, has called Pasadena home for 34 years. He began Blue Moon Aerial Photography in 1987 and has taken almost 50,000 photos of this area. Tom's enthusiasm for the incredible views from aloft has made him a crusader for sharing that breathtaking experience through his photographs.

Cover Photograph

The aerial photograph of the Pasadena peninsula was taken by Thomas Christopher of Blue Moon Aerial Photography, phone 410-437-5000.

Published by Pasadena Business Association, P. O. Box 861, Pasadena, Maryland, 21123-0861. Phone: 410-987-4887

ISBN 0-9674542-0-4

Designed and produced by Fishergate, Inc., Annapolis, Maryland

Printed in the United States of America

Contents

Acknowledgments

It is a pleasure to acknowledge my indebtedness to those who have contributed to this book. Librarians, archivists, historians, government agencies, and many individuals have shared records, photographs, and knowledge of the Pasadena peninsula. Without their help, writing this history would not have been possible. I am especially grateful for the support of the Pasadena Business Association editorial committee. Working with Wendy Harris, Maureen Agro, and George Athas and sharing their enthusiasm for the history of the Pasadena peninsula has been a privilege.

I appreciate the assistance of Jeff Korman, manager of the Pratt Library s Maryland Room; John Beck, Special Collections Assistant at the Kuhn Library, University of Maryland, Baltimore Campus; Emily Murphy at the Maryland State Archives; staff members at the Maryland Historical Society; and librarians at the Annapolis, Harundale, Riviera Beach, and Mountain Road public libraries. Shirley Aaronson at the Maryland Law Library and Rosemary Dodd and Murray Combs at the Anne Arundel County Historical Society s Kuethe Library have been unfailingly helpful.

Donna Ware, Historic Sites Planner at the Anne Arundel County Department of Planning and Code Enforcement; Sherri Marsh, county architectural historian; and

C. Jane Cox, assistant county archaeologist have shared their knowledge of the Pasadena peninsula generously. James G. Gibb, Assistant Director of The Lost Towns Project, has given meticulous attention to the text and made valuable suggestions. Michael Eismeier of the Soil Conservation Service and Stephen Bilicki, Maryland Historic Trust Underwater Archaeologist, have answered questions patiently.

Employees of the Maryland State Highway Administration, the Anne Arundel County Bureau of Highway Administration, the County Board of Education, the County Health Department, and Brian Woodward of the Department of Recreation and Parks have supplied essential information. Deborah Yeater, Superintendent at Lake Waterford Park, has made her files available, and Rick Holt, Superintendent of Downs Park, has shared his research and provided historic photographs.

Representatives of private organizations have answered queries and shared materials. Mary Joe Robl has donated pictures from the Archives of the Girl Scouts of Central Maryland, while members of fire departments, clubs, and churches have recalled their heritage. Carol Cross of the Pasadena Business Association and Carolyn Roeding and Joseph Foran of the Greater Pasadena Council have supplied necessary information. I am indebted to James R. Morrison, president of the Friends of *Hancock's Resolution*, for his help and to Mark N. Schatz, editor of *Anne Arundel History Notes*, for his support and for providing access to photographs from the Society's files.

Many individuals have contributed by searching their memories and their photograph collections. The pictures are the amazing result of the cooperation of residents of the peninsula. James and Mary Calvert and Charles Calvert, descendants of the Hancock and Cook families, have made the contents of their many photograph albums available and have answered innumerable questions patiently. In addition, Charles Calvert has guided our photographer to obscure locations and helped to date old pictures. Emma Schramm has provided information generously and has shared the vast Schramm Collection of memorabilia and photos. Anne Cook Myllo, who is descended from the Calvert, Cook, Chairs, Linsted, and Williams families, has answered many questions and found family photographs. Emma Wade Sanders, whose forebears were the Jenkins and Stinchcomb families, also has provided photographs and information.

I am especially grateful to Jack Kelbaugh, whose grandfather developed Bayside, not only for giving me files of relevant material and many photographs, but also for his constant support and encouragement and his perceptive comments on the text. Jack Mellin, another local historian, offered a choice of his large collection of postcards, as well as other photos. Special thanks go to Walter Kramme for photographing sailing races on the Magothy. Jacques Kelly, author of *Anne Arundel County, A Pictorial History*, kindly contributed photographs from his collection. Milton O. Duvall answered many questions and shared his research on the Civil War period, while Orlando Ridout put into perspective the history of early life on the Pasadena peninsula.

Edward Seipp, John Mason, and Louis Doetsch have been sources of useful information and have offered insights into events on the peninsula. Mildred Everd Oakie, Gerry Strain Hedges, and Marie Christian have shared vivid memories of post-war development. I am indebted also to Herbert Sappington who has supplied information and pictures of the village of Pasadena. Gerald A. Smith's memories of Beachwood

Park have added new information about a black beach resort. In addition, Steve Kimmel of the First Maryland Regiment of the state's official Bicentennial Troop Reenactment group provided a photo of an era when there were no cameras.

People who have contributed significantly include Virginia D. Moore, Jane Pumphrey Nes, Henry A. Schmidt, Senator Alfred Lipin, Clifford Phelps, Debbie Smigovsky, Rayetta Windsor, John Williams, and Harold E. Slanker. I am grateful to Mike Agro, Jr., for making possible the photographs taken from the water. Bob and Hope Meyer, Fran Koslowski, Gladys Rowens, Mildred Strobeck, Clara Dryer Bomhardt, Joan Valenti, Dr. Randall McLaughlin, John Wilson, and Christopher George have provided important information.

Others who shared their time and memories include William Stallings, William G. Rothamel, Marie Angel Durner, James B. Morrison, Ethel Groh Webster Williams, Grace Bottomley Hoenig, Katie Ellison Hyde, Brian Metzbower, Frances Klug Arnold, Clarence and Dorothy Parsley, Philip Beigel, Kenneth Hyde, H.J. Morgereth, Lewis Frazetti, Rosalea Della, Martha Jackowski, John Mogey, Walter Hein, Clinton Gosnell, Clare Edmonston, and B.J. Cullin.

In addition to photographs from the extensive Calvert, Schramm, Kelbaugh, Kelly, and Mellin collections, I appreciate the valuable contributions of Herbert Sappington, Emma Wade Sanders, Janet R. O'Connell, Elisabeth Williams Schmidl, Dolores Klingelhoefer, and Stanley and Anne Cook Myllo. Preston Disney, Joyce Clocker, Lois Chairs Jubb, Senator Al Lipin, Anne Mattson, John Mason, Tom Redmond, Bob and Hope Meyer, John M. Shipley, and Edward Seipp have shared treasured pictures. Bob and Roselle Lawn, Clinton Gosnell, Dale Courville, Harold Belford., Barbara Houck, Helen Neisser, and Dolores Rocklin have provided additional photos.

James Calvert, John Mason, and Emma Schramm have helped immeasurably by reading parts of the text and helping me to avoid mistakes easily made by one who is not a native of the peninsula. I alone am responsible for any remaining errors.

Last, I thank my son, David Cunningham, for patiently guiding me through the pitfalls of word processing.

Isabel Shipley Cunningham
Annapolis, September 1999

Foreword

An unusually large number of self-made people, those who believe in the United States system of free enterprise, reside in Pasadena. Many began working out of their homes or started with a small loan from family. Now highly successful, they choose to remain living in Pasadena and keep their businesses in Pasadena because of its sense of community and family.

Many of these small business people belong to the Pasadena Business Association which sponsored and fostered the publication of this book. The PBA was founded in 1986 by Ed Lauer. The group successfully blocked government funding of a shopping center which, they felt, would hurt the local business people. With a membership of 250 large and small local companies, the PBA has continued to look out for the interests of its members as well as the community.

Monthly informational meetings and numerous opportunities for networking are only the framework of the group. Social activities throughout the year raise funds for scholarships, food drives, high school educational programs, and other community benefits. *Between Two Rivers* marks a milestone for the PBA. The book is a gift of memories and stories to all that call Pasadena home.

The idea for a book was born out of a love for Pasadena. There are the Book Committee members who made the book happen; the Sponsors who paid for production and expenses because they believed in the project; the Patrons who contributed money; and the community residents who loaned photographs, told the stories and pointed the Committee in the right direction—all of these people evidenced an appreciation of the community where they live and work. They realized the importance of recording and preserving the history, current events and future plans of Pasadena for all generations to enjoy.

This book has revealed the wealth of Pasadena—it is rich in friendly people, rich in local businesses, rich in wildlife, and rich in a diversity of small neighborhood communities. *Between Two Rivers* is an attempt to capture the highlights of the history and snapshots of community life in the text and over 250 photographs. It has been a tremendous task and, of course, there are surely things that have been overlooked.

All is not lost since a second book is planned, a textbook that will hold more details of the extensive research already completed. You are encouraged to call the PBA at 410-987-4887 if you have any historical information or current events that you believe should be included in the future book slated for publication in late 2000 or early 2001.

The Pasadena Business Association Book Committee believes in this book and it is our profound hope that it conveys a love for Pasadena to others who also cherish the memories and character of our hometown.

David Blanch
Committee Chairman
—The Idea Started Here

Wendy Harris, *Editor*
Paperwork Solutions

Maureen L. Agro, *Assistant Editor*
Cityline Business Park

George Athas
Editorial Committee; New Photos
Legg Mason

James Anderson, *Financial Committee*
Anderson, Davis & Associates, CPA

Lois Simpson, *Committee Member*
County National Bank

Carolyn Melton, *Committee Member*
Marcom Marketing

(Previous page) Mourning Doves
Photo: Blue Moon Aerial Photography

"To forget our heritage is to be a stream without a source, a tree without a root."

Chinese Proverb

Setting the Stage

Few people who live on the Pasadena peninsula have had an opportunity to learn about its exciting 350-year history. To tell the entire story of the generations who have lived between the Patapsco and Magothy rivers would require many times the space available here; however, this pictorial history will serve as an introduction to the region's rich heritage.

Much has changed on the peninsula during the last three centuries, especially during the last fifty years; yet there is a consistent theme: neighborly people living in communities, people who love their homes and families and work hard to give advantages to their children. Despite repeated waves of new residents during this century, basic values remain unchanged.

Residents of the peninsula have been unfailingly helpful in response to numerous inquiries and requests for photographs. Much of the information they have given so generously will be used in a second book because space limitations prevent its publication now. People have shown devotion to their community by lending nearly two hundred precious old photographs. Choosing among those pictures has been a difficult task.

For the purposes of this book, the Pasadena peninsula is defined according to the boundaries of the 21122 postal zip code. Although Gibson Island is closely connected to the peninsula historically and geographically, its history already has been researched and recorded. In addition, Mary Anne Taylor's recently published *My River Speaks* covers the north shore of the Magothy River so well that this volume can add little new information about that area.

Names of people and places are spelled according to modern usage. Before the first dictionary standardized spelling, words were spelled as the writer heard them. The Robinsons appear in old records as Robossons; the Magothy as Maggothy, Magoty, and Maggotty; and the Patapsco became Patapsico, Pattapscoo, and Potopscoe. In this book, Stoney Creek is Stony Creek, Boons are Boones, and so on.

The author hopes that readers will enjoy *Between Two Rivers* as a pictorial history and as an introduction to the more detailed account of the peninsula that the Pasadena Business Association plans to publish soon.

(Previous page) The head of Back Creek
Photo: James B. Calvert

Between Two Rivers

A Panoramic View
of the
Pasadena Peninsula

Before the White

Man Came

Picture a peninsula bordered by two rivers, a pleasant land blessed with many clear creeks abounding in fish, shellfish, and waterfowl, their sandy shores surrounded by dense woods filled with wildlife and birds. Wolves, black bear, elk, deer, wild turkey, and small game roamed forests that were filed with pines, hollies, and giant oak, chestnut, and tulip trees. Rivers and creeks held an abundance of diamond-back terrapin, oysters, clams, crabs, herring, shad, rock, and many other species of fish. Near the water, the coastal plain was dotted with hills, and the sandy loam soil held red sandstone deposits and traces of various useful minerals. Large white quartzite formations, ancient and rare, occurred here and in only three other places on Earth.

But the peninsula was not entirely uninhabited. For thousands of years, semi-nomadic Algonquian tribes had made seasonal encampments in a region that they knew as a rich hunting and fishing ground. Hunting and gathering parties set out from bases or villages and returned with deer, ducks, geese, fish, clams, and oysters. Native Americans visited the 150-foot-high white rock formation (later called Wishing Rock) to make tools from its extremely hard white quartzite. Archaeological excavations near the Magothy and the Patapsco have revealed barbeque pits, thick layers of oyster shells, sherds from pottery vessels, arrowheads, axes, and spearpoints along the Magothy and the Bodkin, while farmers have found projectile points and other artifacts throughout the peninsula.

During the century before Englishmen settled there, the peaceful Algonquins were challenged by the warlike Susquehannocks. Continued hostilities resulted in the ex-pulsion of the Algonquian tribes by about 1590. When Captain John Smith sailed up the Chesapeake Bay in the early 1600s, he found this region "extreame thicke of small wood as well as trees, and much frequented with wolves, beares, deere, and other wild beasts," but he was surprised that a region so rich in game and marine life was virtually uninhabited.

The ancient White Rocks at the mouth of Rock Creek.

Photo: Marion Warren

(Previous page) Towering ancient outcroppings, now called Wishing Rock. Native Americans used this extemely hard quartzite for making tools and weapons.

Photo: Marion Warren

William Schramm's collection of Native American artifacts found on the Schramm farm.

The Schramm Collection
Photo: Marion Warren

Englishmen Settle

Young Nation

What kind of life did people live in the 110 households on the peninsula between the Patapsco and the Magothy in the closing years of the 18th century? Their homes often were modest two-story log or frame houses with separate kitchens. Nearby would be a tobacco barn, cornhouse, and milkhouse. The typical farm was from 100 to 300 acres, though some were more than 500 acres. Farm owners generally held from ten to fifteen slaves who lived in cabins.

Hancock's Resolution, a home built near Bodkin Point about 1785, is the only surviving stone dwelling of this period in Anne Arundel County. John Hanshaw and his family farmed the property as tenants of the Hancocks for several generations and lived in the one-and-a-half-story house built of native sandstone. The Hancock's stone milkhouse still stands.

The rapid growth of Baltimore following the Revolutionary War had a significant influence on the lives of the people of the peninsula. When Baltimore became a major port that shipped goods to New England and abroad, local residents were ideally situated to take advantage of this market for their lumber and for crops like wheat and corn that were replacing tobacco.

Soon after 1794, Methodists who lived near the Magothy built a log church on

Hancock's Resolution, home of the Hancock family near Bodkin Point. The milkhouse or dairy on the property is shown above.

Collection of Friends of *Hancock's Resolution*, James R. Morrison, President

Mountain Road. As early as 1777, they had gathered to hear Frances Asbury, father of American Methodism, preach in their homes. For more than two centuries, Magothy Methodist Church, the first church on the peninsula, has been a center of community life.

The name of the road that led to the mouth of the Magothy River has puzzled later generations. British settlers expected a coastal plain to be flat like the Eastern Shore of Maryland. Captain John Smith described the western shore of the Chesapeake as "mountainous," and an early land grant on Gibson Island was called *Seven Mountains*. Though even Eagle Hill (the tallest hill on the peninsula) is not one of the fifteen highest points in Anne Arundel County, the early settlers called these hills mountains and the road that led there, Mountain Road.

At the turn of the century, roads were still narrow lanes, often passable only on horseback. In 1799 residents petitioned the legislature for two new roads, one to intersect "the public road leading from Baltimore-

town to the Magothy mountains" and the other to "intersect the mountain road leading to Patapsco ferry." The legislature appointed residents to lay out these roads that were to be funded "by the parties benefitted." Both roads were near the head of the Magothy.

As early as 1810, residents undertook an ambitious project. Using slave labor, they constructed a narrow canal that ran 500

A 1799 tombstone, now behind the third house on the right at Milburn.

Collection of Downs Park, Rick Holt, Superintendent

(Previous page) Dibbins Sandhill Thoroughbred Farm.

Photo: Marion Warren

The 1822 stone lighthouse on Bodkin Point, the first lighthouse in Maryland waters.

Collection of Downs Park, Rick Holt ,Superintendent

yards in a straight line to connect Locust Cove on Bodkin Creek with a pond that opened onto the Chesapeake Bay. Since extensive forests nearby were logged at that time, the purpose of this major project may have been to avoid the passage around Bodkin Point by floating logs through the canal to the Bay.

Once more war with England disturbed tranquil life on the peninsula. When residents saw thirty hostile British vessels enter the Patapsco in April of 1813, the local militia led by Captain Francis Hancock prepared to defend their homes. Especially alarming to families were raiding parties that landed to search for fresh water and food. The defenders served for several weeks at Fort Madison (on Hawkins Point) and patrolled the Bodkin peninsula and Patapsco River shores.

Residents were apprehensive again in August of 1814 when British ships captured vessels on the Patapsco and burned a schooner in Bodkin Creek. When the British fleet approached Fort McHenry in September, Francis Hancock and his company stood ready to signal as soon as they entered the Patapsco. They were to give the alarm from Bodkin Point, using flags by day and burning haystacks by night. Watchers across the Patapsco near North Point were to relay the signal to Fort McHenry.

War did not discourage mining and processing of minerals by the Baltimore Iron Works on the Magothy at the mouth of Blackhole Creek where Dr. Charles Carroll employed a Dutch chemist to manufacture alum and copperas or iron sulphate. This was the first plant in the United States that produced alum. Much slave labor was necessary for this profitable enterprise.

Farming and lumbering continued during the quiet decades that followed the war, and the workboats that were essential to commerce still sailed the creeks and rivers; how-

ever, two major changes occurred. To improve safety for mariners, the United States government bought land for a lighthouse and keeper's house off Bodkin Point. The 35-foot stone lighthouse, the first in Maryland waters, became operational in January of 1822. Sometime after 1830, Methodists who wanted greater lay representation in church affairs left Magothy Methodist Episcopal Church and built White Marsh Methodist Protestant Church where the Lake Shore Fire Department stands.

The 1850 census for the Third District, which includes the peninsula, showed a population of 1,107. Most men were farmers or farm laborers, but there were nine carpenters, two merchants, two doctors, one blacksmith, and one miller. Of the 486 white

Standing near this location on Bodkin Point, Captain Francis Hancock signaled the passing of the British fleet approaching Fort McHenry.

Photo: Marion Warren

children, only 72 attended school. Since farmers no longer grew tobacco, slaveholders held an average of only four slaves.

Most farms varied from 75 to 300 improved acres in 1850, but Henry Dunbar held 700 improved and 900 unimproved acres on Bodkin Neck. Farmers usually owned from one to six horses, one to ten cows, and fifteen to fifty swine. About half grew from 300 to 1,000 barrels of corn as a major crop, while Henry Dunbar, Landy Linsted, and William Williams also grew fruits or vegetables. These progressive farmers led the way to truck farming as the best use of land on the peninsula.

Farms surrounded the only village on the peninsula, Johnson's Store. (The building that was Addison Johnson's store and post office is still standing at 2601 Mountain Road near Armiger Drive.) In addition to the store and post office, nearby were a few homes, the Clinton Academy (a private school on Tick Neck Road), and a public school on Mountain Road east of the village.

An important event in the community was the replacement of the old stone lighthouse at Bodkin Point by a screwpile lighthouse at Seven-Foot Knoll in 1856. Congress appropriated funds for building a wrought-iron lighthouse that was supported by nine cast-iron screwpiles (piles with external threads that were screwed to bedrock). This lighthouse was manned from 1859 until 1948 and was moved to Baltimore harbor in 1988 as an important historic site.

Changes came at Magothy Methodist Episcopal Church in 1859 when the congregation rebuilt across Mountain Road from its original location. At the same time, the black parishioners built Mt. Zion Methodist Episcopal Church south of Mountain Road on one acre that James and Elizabeth Williams deeded to them for a dollar. Theodore W. Kess was lay leader and Sunday School superintendent at Mt. Zion in 1861 when the congregation began the week-long camp meetings that they have continued to hold every year for 138 years.

But a prosperous and peaceful era was ending as conflict over deeply held beliefs led to a devastating civil war between northern and southern states.

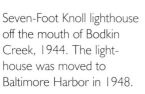
Seven-Foot Knoll lighthouse off the mouth of Bodkin Creek, 1944. The lighthouse was moved to Baltimore Harbor in 1948.

Collection of James Calvert

Historic Magothy Methodist Church, founded
in 1777 and at this site since 1859.

Photo: Marion Warren

Grave of John Hancock, born
1799, died 1853, in Magothy
Church cemetery.

Photo: Blue Moon Aerial Photography

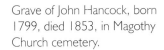

This building served the community known as
Johnson's Store as a general store for many years
and as a post office from 1855 until 1872.

Photo: Marion Warren

Troubled Times

and Recovery

On April 15, 1861, John Barnes of Baltimore sent a letter to Henry Hancock at Bodkin Point with the startling news that war had begun with an attack on Fort Sumter. "The Southern boys have done their work admirably and gained the victory," he wrote. He urged his friend to "get yourself ready to defend the South." Because Anne Arundel County, a Southern-sympathizing county, had voted almost unanimously against the election of Abraham Lincoln in 1860, the federal government imposed martial law when hostilities began, suspending all civil liberties.

Raising troops to fight for the Union was not easy. In 1862 the Provost Marshall sent an enrollment officer with a small detail of Union cavalry to each home in the community called Johnson's Store to find able-bodied men between the ages of 19 and 45. Any man who claimed exemption had to be examined by his doctor. Dr. Samuel Lynch, who had cared for local families faithfully, certified that most of the young men were "diseased" and unable to serve. Others claimed that they were deaf, had a back injury, a broken arm, crippled fingers, or defective vision.

But refusal to serve in the Union Army did not mean that local men were unwilling to fight. John Robinson served as a seaman on a Confederate privateer, the *Tacony*. Other

The grave of Charles Hammond, a Confederate soldier, at Mt. Carmel Church cemetery. The symbol on the stone was used by Maryland's Confederate troops.

Photo: Blue Moon Aerial Photography

orchards in full bloom. Nevertheless, when the new Magothy Methodist Church (built in 1859) burned in 1866, the community raised funds and replaced it without delay.

By 1871 the shift from cereal crops to truck farming was almost complete, with farmers growing vegetables, strawberries, and orchard crops like apples, pears, peaches, and cherries. Baltimore and Philadelphia proved to be such good markets that a merchant bought a steamboat to transport produce from Bodkin Creek to Baltimore.

Having lost their slaves, farmers had trouble finding laborers, especially for picking strawberries. After changes in immigration laws allowed large numbers of Eastern Europeans to emigrate, Polish and Czechoslovakian (called Bohemian) families filled this need [see picture, page 20]. They lived on local farms for six or eight weeks each season and picked berries, peas, and beans. Because a farmer did not receive cash for his crop until it reached the market and because the pickers were not comfortable with written records, farmers paid them with brass checks bearing their initials and a numeral to represent the number of quarts or pecks that had been picked. Farmers redeemed these checks before the pickers returned home.

Confederate volunteers included William Armiger, Ringold Blunt (Blount), William Duvall, Elijah Gray, Zachariah Johnson, John Robinson, and Charles Hammond. Some saw action in the infantry, artillery, cavalry, or with the marines; for some, the record notes only that they "went South."

Others helped the cause by sending supplies to the Confederacy in blockade runners that left the peninsula at night. Jefferson Monroe Cook, whose family owned land from the Magothy to Bodkin Creek, spent large sums on clothing and provisions. Union forces caught blockade runners on Rock Creek and, in April 1862, the Provost Marshall and his squad arrested 24 men there on the charge of intending to go South. Others escaped to a waiting vessel offshore.

After the war times were hard, labor was scarce, and many people were unhappy about the outcome of the struggle. A resident complained that citizens were "taxed to the utmost," but roads were bad and teachers were not paid salaries that they had earned. In addition, an April frost killed apricot

William Landy Cook's picker checks.

Photo: Ann Cook Myllo

Bronze tablet honoring the founders of Magothy Methodist Church, placed in 1998 near the grave of Dorsey Jacobs in the old cemetery across Mountain Road from the present church.

Photo: Marion Warren

When the post office moved from Johnson's Store to Mountain Road at Hog Neck Road in 1872, the postmaster was a member of the Jacobs family, and the village thereafter was called Jacobsville. Dorsey Jacobs, the leading citizen of the community for decades, served as lay preacher at Magothy Church, schoolmaster, and inspector of all county primary schools. He also gave land near the church for the Sons of Temperance Lodge that later housed the Magothy Sunday School and then the overflow from Jacobsville School.

According to the 1878 Hopkins Atlas, four schoolhouses served the peninsula, one on Tick Neck, two on Hog Neck at Rock Point, and one on the Bodkin peninsula. An 1869 deed had provided land for the Rock Point School for white children. In 1874 a black man, Greenberry Johnson, gave land for the

Rock Point School for black children. The Atlas also shows the first bridge over the Magothy. This bridge was almost directly south of Jacobsville. In addition, the atlas identifies Adam Dash's mill at the site of the old mill at Waterford, three Methodist churches, a cemetery, four stores, and a blacksmith shop in the growing community.

Two new Methodist churches began at about this time. In 1875, Virginia Siever sold

The Pasadena Peninsula as it appeared in the 1878 Hopkins Atlas.

Polish pickers at Robert Bottomley's farm in 1909.

Photo: Louis Hine. Special Collections, UMBC

Pupils at Mt. Carmel or Bodkin School Nº 9 in 1895.

Collection of Anne Cook Myllo

The original Mt. Carmel Methodist Church built in 1884 by Jefferson Monroe Cook.

Photo: Marion Warren

land for one dollar to the founders of Piney Grove Methodist Church, a predecessor of Pasadena Methodist Episcopal Church, South. In 1884 Wesley Linthicum gave an oak grove on a knoll where Jefferson Cook built Mt. Carmel Methodist Episcopal Church. Worshipers often came by boat to the county wharf (now Green Gables) and walked to the church. Jefferson Cook drove others from their homes to church in his surrey.

Mount Zion Methodist Church moved to its present site in 1883. Johnsontown nearby was named for the Johnson brothers who hauled the logs that were used to build the church. Freetown, another black community that existed before the war, borders the peninsula. Settlement began in 1845 when James Spencer, a free-born black, bought a tract of land there. Soon other free black men bought adjoining property. Spencer served for three years in the U.S. Army, Colored Troops, during the Civil War. These communities took pride in their independence; they raised their own food, built their own churches, and helped each other in times of need.

But the people of the peninsula would not continue their isolated existence much longer. Soon the wider world would be coming to their shores.

Mt. Zion Methodist Church in 1996. The congregation was formed in 1859 and built at this site in 1883.

Photos: Anne Arundel County Division of Planning

Baltimore Discovers

the Peninsula

Baltimore's discovery of the Pasadena peninsula is a continuing process, but the formation of the Stony Creek Steamship Company and the Rock Creek Steamship Company in 1883 marks its beginning. George Efford and Thomas Bottomley were the principal investors in the Rock Creek Company that ran steamers to the peninsula from Pier 12, Light Street, and from the foot of Broadway. One of their stops was a hotel and resort on Rock Creek called Fairview, advertised in 1890 as "one of the finest beaches for bathing in the State." Fishing and boating were added attractions. Baltimoreans gladly paid 25 cents for a round trip ticket and boarded a steamer that would take them to a beautiful beach where cool breezes blew.

By the mid-1890s, the Rock Creek line served Stony Creek resorts twice on Monday, Wednesday, and Friday and the Rock Creek beaches twice on Tuesday, Thursday, and Saturday. On Sunday the *George W. Johnson* made three trips to both creeks. Wide white sand beaches, picnic tables under trees, and boats for hire lured thousands of Baltimoreans who escaped the heat of the city with loaded picnic baskets.

Though the beaches offered summer entertainment for visitors, the Annapolis *Evening Capital* reported in 1886 that music, games, dancing, and "feasting" were typical

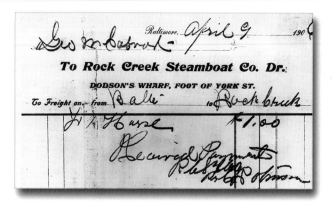

Receipt that G. W. Calvert received from the Rock Creek Steamboat Company in 1906.

Collection of James B. Calvert

activities at gatherings in Jacobsville homes when cold weather brought leisure for farm families. Students at the Clinton Academy gave a musical entertainment that filled the Temperance Hall to capacity in November. But winter also brought freezing temperatures and a wind storm that blew three oyster sloops ashore in Rock Creek. A steam tug that tried to free ice-bound oyster boats in Bodkin Creek was unable to move when ice from the Patapsco River blocked the creek.

Late in March of 1887, the steamer *George W. Johnson* brought fifty Faith Healers to the Marsh farm on Rock Creek. A Baptist elder led twelve candidates into the frigid creek for baptism. Two weeks later, several hundred spectators gathered to see five candidates baptized. About the same time, the pastor of the Magothy Methodist Church attended the Maryland Temperance Alliance meeting and warned that thousands go every Sunday to

Fairview Hotel, a popular destination for vacationers after 1890. The Maryland Yacht Club now occupies this site.

Collection of Jack Kelbaugh

The oyster fleet frozen in Bodkin Creek, February 4, 1936. At such times, the oystermen took the Lake Shore bus to Baltimore to return to their homes on the Eastern Shore.

Collection of James B. & Charles Calvert

(Previous page)
Photo: Blue Moon Aerial Photography

The Sons of Temperence Lodge in 1986. About 1860, Dorsey Jacobs gave the land for this building which served as a community hall and later housed the Magothy Sunday School.

Photo: Anne Arundel County Division of Planning

the city, "that most iniquitous place, worse than Sodom and Gomorrah, . . . to meet ruin and moral degradation."

A disastrous fire burned about 200 acres of woodland belonging to R.W. Chard and E.J. Hines in the spring of 1887. Neighbors fought the blaze for eight or nine hours and finally succeeded in stopping its spread by burning woods some distance ahead of the fire.

Peach and cherry orchards blossomed that spring, and sailboats and small propellor steamers were taking strawberries to the Baltimore market daily by June. A *Sun* reporter wrote that forests had fallen on the peninsula and the whole region had become a beautiful orchard and garden. The delicious peaches, plums, apricots, strawberries, raspberries, watermelons, and cantaloupes, as well as a variety of vegetables grown there had "a more delicate flavor and exquisite richness" than in any other part of the country. Cabbages from the peninsula were unloaded from sloops, bugeyes, and pungees and piled on Bowley's wharf in Baltimore where they were trimmed and boxed and sent to Philadelphia or shipped west.

The opening of the Baltimore and Annapolis Steam Short Line in 1887 gave the communities along the railroad convenient access to Baltimore, but it affected the peninsula only near the village of Pasadena. For most of the region, waterways remained the best route to the city.

Post offices at Armiger, Maynard, and Lake Shore replaced the Jacobsville post office in 1888. James Armiger became postmaster at the Johnson's Store site, changing the name of that crossroads to Armiger. Edward Maynard was postmaster at Maynard on Fairview Beach Road, and the Lake Shore post office was in a store next to the present Lake Shore Fire Company.

In 1890, the Southern Land and Silk Association bought 100 acres that once had been part of the tract called *Waterford*. These people came from California to grow mulberry trees and raise silkworms. According to oral tradition, one of the women in the group named their small village Pasadena after her former home in California. Their hopes were not fulfilled, but the name they gave to their little community now identifies the entire peninsula.

During 1895, the U.S. Army selected Rock Point as one of three sites necessary to the defense of Baltimore. The government bought land there and began to construct a fort in 1899. When the Army Engineers completed a powerful coastal artillery battery emplacement, they named the fort for Major General William Smallwood, commander of the Maryland Line during the Revolutionary War.

Battery Hartshorne, Fort Smallwood, activated in 1902; abandoned after the big guns were dismounted in 1927.

Collection of Anne Arundel County Historical Society

About 1895, William Chairs opened a general store at his home opposite Mt. Carmel Church. This was the first store east of Hog Neck Road. They sold flour and sugar in barrels and big wheels of cheese. A few years later, Harry and Mamie Hancock opened a small store on Bodkin Point. They sold produce, eggs, and salt meat from their farm, as well as cheese, soda crackers in barrels, ginger snaps, rock candy, and chewing tobacco brought by boat from Baltimore. Their customers included pickers, farmhands, and oystermen.

Most land on the peninsula was owned by descendants of early settlers until about 1900 when German immigrants began to buy property there. Even earlier, in 1887,

Augustus Schmidt began to work on a rented farm near Pinehurst. Eventually he saved enough money to buy farms that now form the western half of Riviera Beach and Clearwater Village. Benjamin Klug, another German immigrant, bought 30 acres at the corner of Mountain Road and Waterford Road in 1902. His farmhouse later served as a store, post office, and the Rock Creek and Marley Telephone Company headquarters.

Louis Schramm, who was born in Kurhesse, Germany, bought the 236-acre Richard B. Phelps farm on Mountain Road between Waterford Road and Old Mill Road because his doctor told him that he must give up his job as manager at the Maryland Lime and Cement Company and breathe

Horse pulling a sulky at the home of William Chairs, c. 1910

Collection of Elizabeth Williams Schmidl

Baltimore and Annapolis Railroad car at the West Pasadena siding in 1947. The siding served the Arundel Sand and Gravel Company.

Photo: Robert S. Crockett; Collection of Jacques Kelly.

clean country air. He moved there with his wife and five of their children in 1910. Farming was new to the Schramms, but they learned quickly and soon were growing strawberries, apples, peaches, pears, beans, peas, tomatoes, cucumbers, squash, peppers, cantaloupes, watermelons, sweet potatoes, and field corn.

Sam and Ida Hillman rented a store on Rock Creek in 1908. When they opened a one-room store at the corner of Mountain Road and Hog Neck Road several years later, it was the only store for miles around. The Hillmans sold everything people needed — kerosene, clothing, medicine, and groceries including molasses from a barrel. Sam Hillman died a short time later, but Ida managed the store, made many of the foods that she sold, and took care of three children under six years old. Hillman's Corner is now Pastore's.

Though lumbering had been a profitable business from the time of the first settlers until the 1860s, only isolated hardwood forests remained in 1902 when Wilmer Johnson bought a huge tract of chestnut and oak trees near the Magothy. His son, J. Fred Johnson, supervised cutting lumber there. Later the Johnson Lumber Company used an old landing at Chest Neck Point on the Magothy to ship to Baltimore by barge. Farmers continued to sell timber from isolated parcels of uncultivated land to lumber companies through the 1920s.

Electrification of the Baltimore and Annapolis Railroad in 1907 and completion of the Baltimore and Annapolis Boulevard (Maryland Route 648) in 1912 were important events for Anne Arundel County, but neither had an immediate effect on the peninsula beyond the village of Pasadena. However, a bus from the end of the streetcar

The bus that ran from Brooklyn to Lake Shore is pictured below at Mount Vernon Place Square in Baltimore. The driver, Thomas Gordon, owned the bus in 1912 and 1913. He sold the line to Charles Cook's Cook Transportation Company in 1914. Mr. Cook is pictured on the left in 1914 with his first bus, a converted truck, and his wife Nola, his daughter Constance, and Jeff Chairs.

Photo left: Collection of Elizabeth Williams Schmidl
Photo below: Charles Cook; Collection of Jacques Kelly

line at Brooklyn was important. The enterprise began when a black Baltimorean named Kinnear started a bus line from Brooklyn to Mt. Zion Church. He sold to the Brooklyn and Lake Shore Transportation Company, and Charles Cook bought the line in 1914.

The trip to Baltimore by bus took almost two hours. Removable side-curtains protected riders from dust and rain, but solid rubber tires and wooden seats did not provide a comfortable ride. The driver used buckets of sand and sawdust and pieces of carpet to fill mud holes and potholes. In the winter, pas-sengers carried heated bricks to warm their feet. Justice Thurgood Marshall's father commuted on this bus to his weekend work at the Gibson Island Clubhouse where he was a stern taskmaster to the busboys.

But trains and buses did not displace the small steamers, barges, skipjacks, pungees, bugeyes, and ferry boats that continued to be the mainstay of transportation and commerce within the peninsula and beyond its borders. The steamers that ran continually to and from Baltimore, picking up passengers and commodities at public and private

The *Rhoda Virginia*, Henry Alfred Cook's market boat, named for his wife, Rhoda Virginia Hancock Cook.

Collection of Henry Alfred Schmidt, the Cooks' grandson

wharves, have been called an early form of rapid transit and the chief cause of the region's prosperity.

Boats with special functions were the buy boats and market boats. Watermen could sell their catch to buyers waiting in buy boats anchored in deep water. A farmer could load a scow with produce and use a long pole to push the scow to the buy boat anchored off-shore. Some farmers owned market boats that took their produce to Baltimore. Alfred Cook's market boat, the *Rhoda Virginia*, was a sixty-foot pungee built in 1902; George W. Calvert's later market boat, a motor freighter called the *Calvert*, had a swinging boom, one mast, and a pilot house.

The oyster dredges that came from the Eastern Shore were a familiar sight along the Bodkin peninsula until the 1930s. In 1905 a U.S. Marshall aboard the revenue cutter *Windsor* inspected dredge boats off the Magothy because he had heard that some of the crew had been "shanghaied." Though some men admitted that they had been shanghaied, they refused to be rescued because they were glad to have a job and regular pay.

The whistle of the steamboat continued to announce the arrival of hundreds of excursionists at resorts like Colonial Beach or Fairview Park. By 1908 the Rock Creek Steamship Company had added the *Clio* and the 77-foot propeller-driven *Severn* to its fleet. In contrast, workboats sailed to Baltimore at dusk, carrying produce from private

BELOW: The steamer *Clio* on the Patapso River at Clearview. RIGHT: The *Severn*, a 77-foot steamboat built in Baltimore in 1891, bringing crowds to the beach.

Below: Collection of Jack Kelbaugh
Right: Marion E. Warren Collection, Maryland State Archives

and county wharves. In the winter, barges and motor freighters like the *Blandford* hauled manure from dairies and streetcar barns to provide the farmer with fertilizer, an essential for growing fruits and vegetables.

As early as 1910, seed catalogues featured the green-meat cantaloupe that Robert Bottomley originated on his Fort Smallwood Road farm. "This is without doubt the best yet. It produces more and better fruit and commands a higher price than any other cantaloupe on the market today," one catalogue claimed. Large, sweet, resistant to blight, and a fine shipper, the "Bottomley" (along with Anne Arundel's other famous green-meat cantaloupes, Adam Neidert's "Knight" and John Dick Shipley's "Long John") dominated the Baltimore market for decades.

About 1918 Louis Schramm developed the slightly earlier and larger "Schramm" cantaloupe, a selection from "Bottomley." The "Schramm" was grown widely around Norfolk, Virginia. Hundreds of thousands of green-meat melons reached the Baltimore market from the Alfred Stinchcomb, Louis Schramm, Augustus Schmidt, Gustavus Jenkins, Henry A. Cook, and Charles. H. Calvert farms. On one occasion during the 1920s, George Jenkins sent twelve loads of melons to market by truck and shipped 2,500 baskets on his scow.

BELOW: Pickers working in a field on Robert Bottomley's farm in 1909.
RIGHT: John Dick Shipley at his farm near Bayside Beach watching men load his 1928 Model AA Ford truck with "Long John" cantaloupes, which he originated.

Photo below: Louis Hine. Special Collections, UMBC
Photo right: Collection of John M. Shipley

William L. Cook packing cantaloupes with his
1927 Chevrolet truck in the background.

Photo: A. Aubrey Bodine, in *The Sun*
Collection of Stanley and Anne Cook Myllo

Summertime In Anne Arundel

A photograph by A. Aubrey Bodine

Scenes on William Chairs's farm opposite Mt. Carmel Church in 1910. Bottom picture shows glass-covered hot beds that protected seedlings in early spring.

Collection of Elizabeth Williams Schmidl

TOP: William L. Cook on his farm wagon with Urma Williams Cook and friends, about 1910.

Collection of Anne Cook Myllo

CENTER: Harry Williams hauling cantaloupes to the county wharf in 1914. Photo taken by Margie Chairs, who married Harry Williams in 1914.

Collection of Elizabeth Williams Schmidl

BOTTOM: Men clearing Charles Hancock Calvert's field in 1915. Mr. Calvert is in the center background.

Collection of James B. Calvert

J. Oliver Calvert and Charles H. Calvert aboard the *Belle*, a 23-foot deadrise built by their father, George Washington Calvert, about 1910.

Collection of Charles Calvert

Businesses related to farming flourished. Instead of marketing produce in Baltimore, corn, beans, and tomatoes were canned on the Schultz and Bottomley farms and at the Adams cannery beside the Pasadena railroad station. Until about 1925, Swift's burlap bag factory made bags that farmers used by the hundreds. Farmers often trapped and fished for income during the winter and sent their catch to Baltimore. They also built their own boats like George W. Calvert's *Belle*, a 23-foot deadrise with a 6.5 horsepower engine. Calvert also built a marine railway beside his wharf on Back Creek, using a stump puller to pull customers' boats up the ramp.

Blacksmiths were essential in the days of horse-drawn vehicles. Tom Stallings, who had learned his trade from his predecessor, Edward J. Hines, built a blacksmith shop on Mountain Road at Lake Shore Road in 1912. Stallings enjoyed shoeing horses, building and repairing farm wagons, and even building boats. He made every part of a wagon, even the iron wheel rims. Robert Gray had a blacksmith shop at the entrance of what is

Charles Hancock Calvert's farm truck loaded with burlap bags in 1934. The bags are filled with cans used to start cantaloupe and tomato seeds.

Collection of James B. Calvert

Label from a can of tomatoes hand-packed by J. C. Schultz, Pasadena.

Collection of Jack Kelbaugh

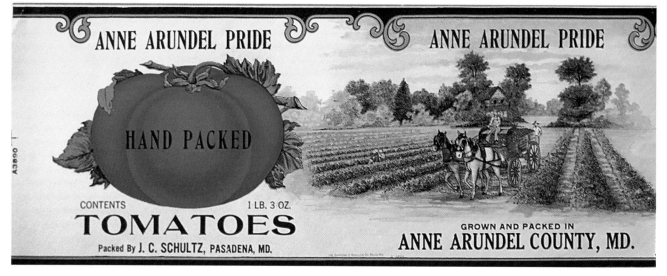

Dr. Billingslea's bill for professional services to the Henry Alfred Cook family, 1910.

Collection of Henry Alfred Schmidt, his grandson

now Chesterfield, and Charles Brown was the blacksmith at Pasadena. Farmers like Henry Alfred Cook and George Calvert had their own blacksmith shops on their farms, which were nearly self-sufficient.

James S. Billingslea became the community's family doctor in 1904 when he was just 22 years old. He rode horseback to make daily house calls that cost two dollars or less. Although he moved to Glen Burnie in 1919, he continued to take care of families on the peninsula until the 1960s.

About 1910 Melville Dunlap, a retired teacher, lay preacher, and Justice of the Peace, lost valuable papers when his home burned. Determined that he never would suffer such a loss again, Squire Dunlap built a house and separate office entirely of pressed tin. When Turf Valley on Tick Neck was developed in 1984, this unique house was destroyed.

A fire, a new telephone exchange, and a new bridge brought changes during the next two years. When the Schramm's barn burned in 1911, the firefighters' only equipment was a horse-drawn wagon carrying a large barrel of water. In 1912 the Armiger telephone exchange headquarters moved to the

The Tin House that Squire Dunlap built on Tick Neck Road about 1910.

Courtesy of *Anne Arundel History Notes*

His grandchildren watch as William Thomas Stallings shoes a horse at the shop he opened in 1912.

Collection of Anne Cook Myllo

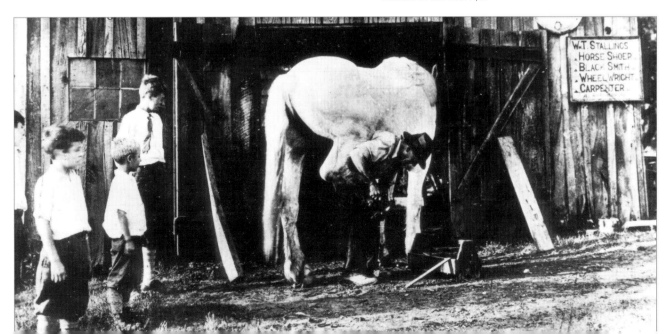

36   BETWEEN TWO RIVERS

Frances Schramm, telephone operator in 1914, when the Armiger exchange was in the Schramm home.

The Schramm Collection

Schramm home after the Chesapeake and Potomac Telephone Company bought the Rock Creek and Marley Telephone Company. Frances and Emma Schramm, Louis Schramm's daughters, were the operators until 1932. Also in 1912, a wooden bridge with wooden sides spanned Stony Creek. This bridge remained in service until 1946.

Anne Arundel County expected public-spirited members of the community to give land for schools and build the buildings. Alfred Stinchcomb gave land for the Tick Neck School where the children observed Arbor Day with recitations, songs, tree planting, and awards for regular attendance to Elva and Theodore Stinchcomb. When George W. Calvert built a new school at Rock Point at the turn of the century, the county gave him the abandoned school as payment, and he moved it to his home to use as a summer kitchen.

The county government improved local roads by buying great quantities of oyster shells from canning houses and having work crews spread a deep layer over the main roads. On the peninsula, barges brought the shells to local wharves. Wagon wheels gradually pulverized the shells; until that happened, the fragments were hard on horses' hooves.

Stony Creek Bridge, November 16, 1946.

Photo: Jacques Kelly, *News American*

Charles Hancock Cook with his wife and neighbors at Rock Point School #5 in 1918. Mr. Calvert mowed the school grounds with a two-horse mowing machine. The hole in the foundation was used to store coal for the stove.

Collections of James B. and Charles Calvert

Annie Stinchcomb and a friend in a buggy about 1910.

Collection of Emma Jenkins Wade Sanders

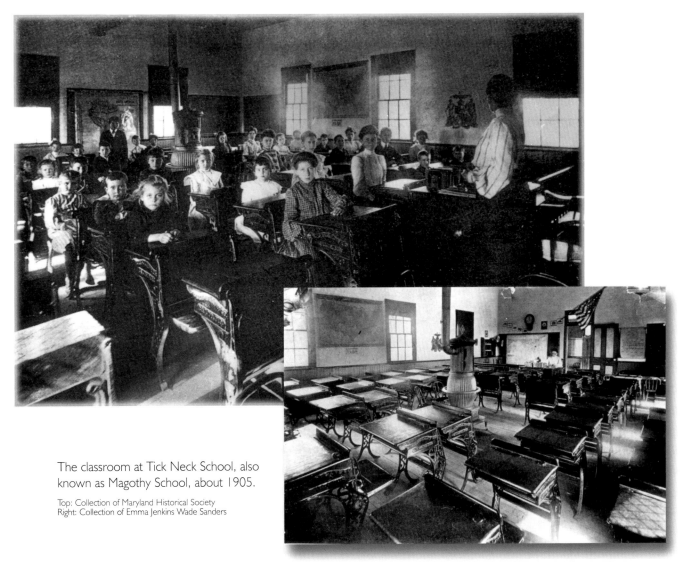

The classroom at Tick Neck School, also known as Magothy School, about 1905.

Top: Collection of Maryland Historical Society
Right: Collection of Emma Jenkins Wade Sanders

Pasadena Elementary School about 1920.

The Schramm Collection and Pasadena School

At the western end of the peninsula, Elzey and Ellen Wade owned a store that served Pasadena and Elvaton and housed the Elvaton post office from 1909 until 1914. As the community grew, the School Commissioners built a one-room school in the village of Pasadena in 1911. Like other schools at that time, it had a vestibule for hanging coats, double desks, and slates for writing but no running water. When the county replaced it with a four-room shingled school in 1924, the Schramms bought the old school and added it to their home. Methodists at Pasadena met in homes and at the school until 1917 when they merged with the Piney Grove congregation and built the Pasadena Methodist Episcopal Church, South.

For decades, a source of winter income for local farmers was the sale of charcoal made

Wade's Store served served Pasadena and Elvaton from the early 1900s until the mid thirties.

Collection of Emma Jenkins Wade Sanders

by burning pine wood slowly. Walter J. Phelps, whose farm was at Lake Shore, cut pine in four-foot lengths and built so-called charcoal pits, actually ricks, fifteen feet in diameter. He and his son, Clifford Phelps, covered the tall structure with sod to make it airtight, except for air vents used to regulate temperature as it burned. For several weeks, they blocked some of the vents if it burned too quickly. Then they let the rick cool for a week before removing the first "draw." After filling burlap bags with the charcoal, they hauled it to Baltimore in two-horse wagons. The horses had a hard time pulling the wagon through snow or over Cedar Hill near Brooklyn when the road was icy. If a horse fell, they had to put a blanket under his feet and get him up again.

As war began in Europe, the Armiger, Maynard, and Lake Shore post offices closed and were replaced in 1914 by the Pasadena post office with its easy access to trains that delivered mail. From that time on, the entire peninsula between the Magothy and Patapsco became the Pasadena peninsula. Albert B. Clark. the first postmaster, built a tiny addition to his home near the railroad station to serve as the post office. When a heavy snow fell, he dug a path through several feet of snow to pick up mail at the station. Herbert Groh was the rural carrier who served a long route along the peninsula until he entered military service in World War I.

After 1913 Charles and Henry Efford, sons of George Efford, became managers of the Rock Creek Steamship Company and Fairview Park. The park featured amusements including a penny arcade, bowling, a merry-go-round, and a dance pavilion. Among the scheduled stops on the Rock Creek line were Fairview, Colonial Beach, and Heintzman's Cottage Grove. Excursion steamers like the *William Linthicum* stopped at North Ferry Point on the Magothy.

Heintzman's Cottage Grove, a popular beach resort.

Collection of Jack Kelbaugh

The carousel at Fairview Park.

Collection of Jack Kelbaugh

Patrons of Fairview enjoyed cruising on this boat.

Collection of Jack Kelbaugh

Several Baltimore-based groups sponsored summer camps on the Magothy. The Grachur Club, young men and boys from Grace Methodist Church near Bolton Hill, bought property on Cockey Creek in 1914. Led by their Sunday School teacher, Claude B. Whitby, they raised money to build a clubhouse. To reach their camp, they took the train to Robinson station, walked to the river, and crossed the Magothy by canoe. They were responsible for assigned camp chores, but they found plenty of time for swimming, canoeing, and games.

The Girl Scouts established Camp Whippoorwill on the Magothy in 1918 on what had been part of Captain Robinson's farm. His three-story farmhouse became their headquarters. The girls traveled by train to Jones Station, by cart to South Ferry Point, and by ferry across the Magothy on the *Diana*. They wore white middie blouses, black bloomers, black ties, and knee stockings. Swimming, canoeing, and sailing were among their favorite activities.

Camp Milbur on Cornfield Creek began in 1921 when two military men, Captain Miller and Captain John Burgess (hence the name, Milbur) founded a camp that aimed to build character through discipline. The boys wore uniforms, took part in military drills, and responded to bugle calls, but they also enjoyed swimming, canoeing, baseball, and other activities. To reach the camp, the boys traveled from Baltimore by train and ferried across the Magothy on motor launches like the *Desdemona* or *Maid of the Mist*.

The waterfront at Camp Wippoorwill.

Collection of Jack Kelbaugh

TOP: Captain Robinson's home on the Magothy, later Girl Scout headquarters at Camp Whippoorwill.
Collection of Howard Belford

CENTER: Saluting the flag at Camp Milbur, Cornfield Creek.
Collection of Jack Kelbaugh

BOTTOM: The ferry at Milbur on Cornfield Creek.
Collection of Lois Chairs Jubb

LIPIN'S CORNER

Established in 1918 by John Lipin, and devoted to the ever-growing automobile traffic of Anne Arundel County.

Good Gasoline   Good Tires
Good Accessories
ANNAPOLIS BOULEVARD AND MOUNTAIN ROAD

Lipin's Corner where Mountain Road left the Baltimore-Annapolis Boulevard, a landmark for vacationers on their way to the beach.

Collection of Senator Alfred Lipin

For those who came to the peninsula by car, Lipin's Corner was the landmark where they left the main road to Annapolis and drove down Mountain Road to the beaches. John Lipin opened a gas station there in 1918, selling gasoline, tires, and accessories. His business grew to include the sale of food and drinks. Later, Lipin's Corner was known for massive traffic jams on Sunday evenings when everyone tried to return home from the beach at the same time. While long lines of cars waited to enter the Baltimore and Annapolis Boulevard, passengers had time to go into Lipin's store and buy a cold drink.

Baltimoreans who came to the Pasadena peninsula for a day at the beach had glimpsed Utopia. When Augustus Smith began to sell lots on the west side of what became Riviera Beach, they had an opportunity to fulfill their dream of owning a place near the water. His first sale in 1914 was to Mayor Broening, who built a summer home

just twelve miles from City Hall. Where Green Haven is now, Charles M. Christian sold small lots at a reasonable price. His ads about "the pride of possession" and "the joys of living" led families to buy land where they could pitch a tent and spend the weekend fishing and swimming.

In 1918 the United States entered the war to make the world safe for democracy, and many men from the Pasadena peninsula served their country in the trenches in France. Herbert Groh, who had been the Pasadena mail carrier from 1914 until he enlisted, died in a seaplane accident while delivering mail for the U.S. Navy. During the war, prejudice against German immigrants forced Gustavus A. Lotze to move his florist and nursery business from Glen Burnie to Long Hill near Lipin's corner. For many years, he imported and sold the newest and finest varieties of flowers there.

The terrible flu epidemic in 1919 forced

Christmas greeting sent to patrons by Herbert E. Groh, Pasadena mail carrier who died in a seaplane accident while delivering mail for the U.S. Navy during World War I.

Collection of Ethel Groh Webster Williams

the closing of schools at Pasadena and Jacobsville. Also in 1919, Baltimore City attempted to dispose of its garbage by establishing a piggery on 160 acres at what is now Ventnor. The plan was to take garbage there by barge and feed it to 15,000 pigs. Forty local residents filed a lawsuit against the city, but the City Solicitor ruled that a piggery would not depreciate property values. Before residents could file an appeal, the pigs became ill and some died, the manager of the piggery absconded with $15,000 belonging to the city, and Baltimore returned to incineration and landfill to dispose of garbage.

The end of the war in November 1918 brought a feeling of optimism to the United States and to the people living between the Magothy and the Patapsco. They faced the 1920s with high hopes.

Advertisement for lots at Green Haven.

Collection of Jack Kelbaugh

The Roaring Twenties,

Depression, and War

A decade of peace and prosperity during the 1920s was a productive time for farmers, realtors, and builders. Many Baltimoreans wanted to buy land near the water, and developers were eager to accommodate them. German and Polish families from south and east Baltimore saved hard-earned dollars to make monthly payments on small lots in Outing Park (Green Haven), while well-to-do families built comfortable homes in restricted waterfront communities like Pinehurst on the Chesapeake Bay.

Stewart and Ernest Robinson began to develop Pinehurst-on-the-Bay as a summer colony in 1922. The Pinehurst Company had to approve all building plans in this gated community. Early residents included doctors and successful businessmen from Baltimore City and Baltimore County. Near the community beach were bathing facilities, swings, picnic tables, a baseball diamond, a tennis court, and the Tea House where adults enjoyed dinners and card parties.

Charles M. Christian, the son of a doctor, formed the Outing Park Development Company with the idea that a family with a modest income should be able to live near the waterfront. He advertised 25- by 100-foot lots in what became Green Haven for $20 to $50 each, with "terms to suit any buyer." His newsletter, *The Green Haven Hash*, reminded readers of the benefits of owning land with access to the water "far away from the noise, smoke, and cares of the city."

A stucco house.

PINEHURST IN 1929

Collection Janet R O'Connell

The beach and sliding board.

An oyster-shell road.

The bathhouse
and parking lot.

(Previous page) Mother's Garden at Downs Park.
Photo: Marion Warren

Postcard advertising lots at
Outing Park, later Green Haven.

Collection of Jack Kelbaugh

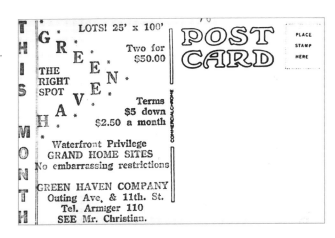

When they learned that a five dollar deposit and small weekly payments would buy a lot at Outing Park, many Baltimoreans were able to fulfill their dreams. Their holiday began when they boarded a steamer Friday evening and left the hot city for the ride down the Patapsco. All the families who owned lots in the development were friends. They stayed in tents or shacks at first, but they were happy as they enjoyed swimming, fishing, and crabbing.

Water pollution was not a concern when the developer advertised that Outing Park was bordered for half a mile by a stream of pure water and the land near the stream was "porous with abundant shade, making it especially suitable for raising poultry. Hundreds of chickens are raised in the Park each year, and there is an excellent local market for both chickens and eggs." One man

GREEN HAVEN IN THE 1920s

Beach scene.
Collection of Jack Mellin

Fourth Street, now 204th Street.
Collection of Jack Kelbaugh

Steamer discharging passengers.
The Schramm Collection

Advertisement for the "Suits Us"
model house in Riviera Beach.

made more money selling poultry products for six years than he had made in twenty years as a bookkeeper in Baltimore.

Near Bodkin Point in 1924, the Bayside Beach Development Company was advertising the view across the Chesapeake, a sandy beach, saltwater bathing, boating, fishing, and cool breezes, "an ideal spot to build your bungalow and make your dreams come true." Charles Rittenhouse managed sales, and his partner, Emory Archer Kelbaugh, was the building contractor. During the booming twenties, his carpenters came to work wearing silk shirts. Restrictions in deeds enabled the developers to approve all building plans, including exterior paint color. This sedate community attracted people like the Schluderburgs (of Esskay) and author Swepson Earle. Building continued on a reduced scale there, even during the Depression.

When T.W. and Charles Pumphrey formed the Riviera Beach Development Company in 1924, their advertisements encouraged buying a home where the entire family could enjoy life while making payments that were lower than rent. Options included "The Chesapeake," "The Riviera," and the modest "Suits Us" that cost $1,250, payable at $25 each month. A sandy beach, excellent harbors, and a fully equipped playground were additional lures. By 1927 ads mentioned tennis and basketball courts, a baseball diamond, and an "environment of refinement." Also in 1927, the Consolidated Gas and Electric Light and Power Company extended its lines to Riviera Beach.

In addition to Green Haven, Charles Christian developed High Point nearby. Early summer homes there gradually were converted into small but well-kept permanent homes. The owners usually worked in Baltimore. Steven J. Everd, a building contractor who had been sales manager at Outing Park, developed Clearwater Village.

Edward and Chester Seipp on Mission Street, Pasadena, in the 1920s.

Collection of Edward Seipp

Though many Baltimoreans wanted to live near the water, others were attracted by Pasadena's location on the Baltimore and Annapolis Railroad. After military service in World War I, Joseph Groh began to build homes there. He and John Appleton built most of the houses in the village of Pasadena. Before the community was split by a dual highway, everyone enjoyed the annual carnival that temporarily closed Mission Street. When John Appleton founded Pasadena Water Works in 1925, only six homes were on the line that supplied water for indoor plumbing.

By the late 1920s, new homeowners lived in dozens of small developments and individual homes along the Magothy, the Patapsco, and their tributaries. Most residences were summer homes, but affordable automobiles and better roads soon would enable people to live near the water throughout the year. Major advances were the rebuilding of the bridge over the Magothy and paving Mountain Road, a project done in four segments and completed in 1928. Secondary roads remained unpaved, dusty or muddy, according to the season.

William H. Rothamel built this 17-room log cabin at Pea Patch Point on the Magothy during the winters of 1920 and 1921.

Photo: Marion Warren

The lack of good roads did not affect the beaches and resorts. Steamships continued to bring crowds to George Cook's Alpine Beach, Heintzman's Cottage Grove, McCoach's Colonial Beach, Efford's Fairview Park, Grantlin's Maryland Beach, and Fort Smallwood Park. The War Department had closed Fort Smallwood in 1926, dismounted the guns, and sold the fort to Baltimore City for use as a park. Beginning in 1931, thousands of people came to Fort Smallwood Park by steamer and by automobile. Those who reached the beaches by steamer did not realize that farms surrounded all these resorts.

Brown's Grove, on Rock Creek near the end of Colony Road, was the only black resort to have its own steamers. Captain George Brown, a black man who had come to Baltimore penniless in his youth, owned three excursion boats, the *Starlight*, *Avalon*, and *Newbill*. They made repeated trips down the Patapsco to Brown's Grove on weekends. Beginning with refreshment stands, a picnic grove, and bathhouses, Captain Brown added a merry-go-round, a racerdip ride, a midway, and a dancing pavilion with a good band. After midnight on July 5, 1938, fire broke out in the racerdip (a roller-coaster). The blaze had reached spectacular proportions when the Riviera Beach and Orchard Beach Fire Companies arrived. By morning, all that remained was smoldering rubble.

RIGHT: One of several steamboats that served the beachgoing public in the 1920s and 1930s.
The Schramm Collection

BELOW: Bathers enjoying the wide expanse of sand at Maryland Beach.
Collection of Jack Kelbaugh

The pier where excursion boats docked.
Collection of Jacques Kelly

Swimmers could rent bathing suits in 1930.
Photo: *News American*

A daring two-piece bathing suit attracts attention.
Collection of Jacques Kelly

FORT SMALLWOOD PARK IN THE 1930S AND 1940S

Bathers enjoying the water in 1947.
Photo: *News American*

The hotel at New Altona Beach on the west bank of Stony Creek.

Collection of Jack Kelbaugh

Postcard promoting Heintzman's Cottage Grove.

Collection of Jack Mellin

Dance pavilions were popular during the twenties and thirties when young people danced the foxtrot, jitterbug, and Big Apple. The largest dance hall on the Pasadena peninsula was the two-story pavilion built by the Robinsons on Pinehurst's South End Beach in 1928. Lighted by Japanese lanterns and encircled by tables, the raised maple dancing surface measured 75 by 50 feet. On Wednesday and Saturday nights, popular bands came from Baltimore to play at the dances. The building, which extended over the Bay, was surrounded by a screened porch where older people sat in rockers watching the boats on the Bay and listening to the music.

The Effords built a dance pavilion at Fairview in the 1920s. Heintzman's Cottage Grove offered a partially enclosed and partially screened dance pavilion beside Rock Creek where popular bands from Baltimore played. Residents of Pasadena enjoyed dancing at Chestnut Grove at the intersection of West Pasadena Road and Jumpers Hole Road, and a few recall a pavilion on the hill above the north bank of Lake Waterford near the Baltimore and Annapolis Boulevard.

After Gustav and Samuel Kurtz opened Kurtz's Pleasure Beach in 1933, they built an octagonal dance pavilion near the waterfront. Like their father who had emigrated from Austria, they were bakers and had bakery stalls in six markets in Baltimore. During the Depression, they saved enough money to buy land on the water, but so many of their

The pavilion with 50'×75' dance floor that the Robinsons built at Pinehurst in 1928.

Collection of Janet R. O'Connell

Entrance sign at Kurtz Pleasure Beach and sailboats racing nearby.

Left: Collection of Tom Redmond
Right: Collection of Jack Mellin

friends came to visit them there that they decided to open a resort. Soon it was their only business. The Kurtz pavilion is the sole survivor of the dance halls of the thirties.

The decade of the twenties was the era of prohibition and bootleggers. Some residents of the peninsula operated stills and speakeasies, while others were runners who delivered to customers. Stills along the Magothy, on Bodkin Neck, and near Lake Waterford produced the whiskey that moonshiners took to Baltimore and Washington. Runners often

Early view of Angel's store on Mountain Road.

Collection of Tom Redmond

were protected by politicians, but federal agents raided stills and destroyed them with dynamite. Stories are told of a boiler that hung from tree branches after agents blew up a local still and of a narrow escape from agents by rowboat. The whiskey made on the Pasadena peninsula was so much in demand that stills continued to operate after the repeal of prohibition in 1934.

Most local residents ignored stills and speakeasies and devoted their energy to their farms, jobs, and businesses. On the corner of Mountain Road at Waterford Road opposite his father's store, William Klug began to sell vegetables from his farm at a roadside stand about 1919. In 1929 he and his wife, Elsie, opened a Shell gas station and a general store featuring Elsie Klug's pies. By the mid-twenties, Jim Jubb owned a store east of Hillman's. Later his wife Effie was in charge of the store in their home.

In 1923 Samuel and Marie Angel opened a summertime refreshment stand on Mountain Road at Lake Shore. In an 8- by 15-foot space, they sold homemade bottled drinks, cookies, candy, bread, home-made ginger muffins, snuff, and cigarettes. The next year,

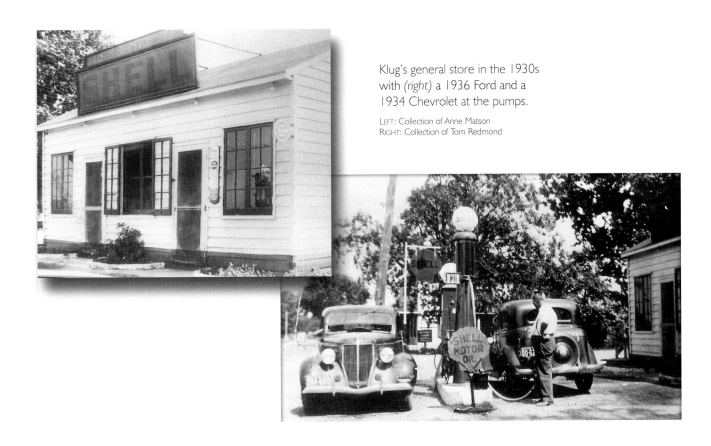

Klug's general store in the 1930s
with *(right)* a 1936 Ford and a
1934 Chevrolet at the pumps.

LEFT: Collection of Anne Matson
RIGHT: Collection of Tom Redmond

Posed picture at a still
near the Magothy.

Photo: A. Aubrey Bodine
Peale Museum Collection, Baltimore

they built a home that housed an all-year grocery store, but they had to rebuild when Mountain Road was relocated in 1928.

At Lake Waterford, William Woole and his sister, Henrietta Woole Windsor, operated a business on property their father had bought in 1912. The elder William Woole, director of Druid Hill Park in Baltimore, chose Lake Waterford for his retirement, built a home there, and stocked the lake with bluegill, bass, and pike. In 1927 his son and daughter built a concession stand near the lake and rented log cabins to fishermen and vacationers. Among their patrons were the families of midshipmen who stayed at Lake Waterford during Graduation Week.

During the twenties, Captain Henry Wickert owned an ice plant and store at the head of Bodkin Creek. He brought supplies from Baltimore in his boat called *No Name*

for his store and the Hancock store. In 1927 William Schmidt, who owned Tall Oaks Farm at the end of Route 100, sold produce at a roadside stand construted of canvas supported by poles. Several years later, he built a sandstone stand on Mountain Road. In the early thirties, Charles Williams opened a gas station at the corner of Mountain Road and Long Point Road.

In 1931 Isadore Hillman enlarged his mother's store and later added an Amoco filling station, but Hillman's still opened at six a.m. and stayed open until the last customer had been served in the evening. When the terrible hurricane of 1933 struck the area, Gussy Hillman recalls that summer residents of Bayside Beach sought shelter at the store and spent the night there. The Hillmans owned the store until the late 1960s.

Painting of William Woole's home at Lake Waterford in 1920.
Collection of Rayetta Windsor

At Lake Waterford in 1927, a concession stand operated by William Woole, Jr., and Henrietta Woole Windsor and row-boats on the lake.

Collection of Rayetta Windsor

William Schmidt's road-side produce stand on Mountain Road, opened in 1927.

Collection of Henry Schmidt

Lett's Whiteford Inn on Baltimore-Annapolis Boulevard in Pasadena , 1927.

Collection of Anne Arundel County Historical Society

John Wilson, Sr, and his wife May opened their Amoco service station on Mountain Road in 1934 and moved it a short distance down the road to its present location in 1937. Mrs. Wilson sold home-grown vegetables, ftuit, and fancy frying chickens there, and the station became a gathering place for residents of Lake Shore. Customers depended on the Chairs' store and Joseph and Andy Coach's grocery store on Hog Neck that delivered purchases by horse and wagon. At the western end of the peninsula, Lett's Whiteford Inn on Annapolis Boulevard sold refreshments, and Elzey Wade's general store survived until the mid-thirties.

The twenties continued to be a profitable time for farmers. Though trucks replaced wagons elsewhere, many farmers on the peninsula still sent their produce to Baltimore by boat. Robert Bottomley, Oliver Duvall, and John Neidert shipped from Bottomley's wharf at Tar Cove on Rock Creek; Sam Dunlap and James Armiger had wharves on Bodkin Creek; Warren Cook, George Jenkins, and Charles (Buck) Jubb used the landing at the end of Ventnor Road; and Captain Ed Deale's bugeye, the *John R. Benton*, stopped at the county wharf on Wharf Creek and at Cook's wharf for produce from the Henry A. Cook, Harry Hancock, and Charles H. Calvert farms on Hog Neck. The Schramms shipped from the county wharf at Green Haven, but they used trucks too. Along the Magothy, bugeyes like John Dougherty's *Florence* picked up fruits and vegetables at Cornfield Creek, Pea Patch Point, and Black Hole Creek.

John Wilson's service station, 1937.

Collection of John Wilson

Loading cantaloupes on Captain Ed Deale's bugeye, the
John R. Benton, at Charles Hancock Calvert's wharf in 1931.

Collection of James B. Calvert

The *John R. Benton*,
Captain Deale's market
boat, on Back Creek.

Collection of Charles Calvert

Louis Schramm, Sr., with family members and
friends admiring the Schramm's first truck in 1920.

The Schramm Collection

The long driveway to Henry Alfred Cook's
house on Bodkin Creek, 1932.
Collection of James B. Calvert

men hauled in at ebb tide with 1,000 feet of rope. He smoked fish in a smoke house, stored them in his ice house, and sold his catch to Freeburger in the fish market in Baltimore. His son George carried on the business after his death. Milton Fick, Robert Gray, Buck Kaiser, and Vince Bailey and his brother supplemented their income by fishing and crabbing, selling locally or shipping to Baltimore from Cook's wharf.

As population increased, more churches served the people of the peninsula. Neighbors organized a Methodist Sunday School in Mrs. Cosden's home in what became Green Haven as early as 1911. The church that became the Community Methodist Church of Riviera Beach met first on Anne Riley's porch and then in the Stadiger's garage. They built in 1921 and laid the cornerstone of an enlarged church in 1925. St. Jane Frances Roman Catholic Church on Church Road at Tick Neck Road in Riviera Beach was completed in 1924, but Saint Rose of Lima Catholic Church in Brooklyn had begun a mission there years before.

Though farming was the main employment on the Pasadena peninsula, a few men worked as watermen. John Dreyer made his living from the water all through the year. He built his own boats at Hickory Point on Sillery Bay and fished the Magothy and the Chesapeake Bay with six or seven pound nets. He also used a seine that eight or ten

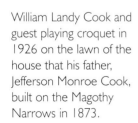

William Landy Cook and guest playing croquet in 1926 on the lawn of the house that his father, Jefferson Monroe Cook, built on the Magothy Narrows in 1873.

Collection of Anne Cook Myllo

where it hung against a piling. But he always delivered the mail, even in deep snow when he used a horse and sleigh. After he injured his hand permanently when he stopped to help a stranded motorist, he continued as before with the use of only one hand. When he retired in 1961, the entire community joined in honoring him at a surprise testimonial dinner.

Family doctors also served the entire community faithfully. When Dr. Leo Breit left his homeland during the Russian Revolution and came to the Bodkin community, he knew no one there and had no transportation. William Landy Cook would lend his car when Dr. Breit needed to make house calls until neighbors contributed money to enable him to buy a car. Dr. Breit cared for residents of the peninsula from 1923 until 1948.

The Great Depression of the 1930s followed the period of optimism, silk shirts, and shiny new cars. After the stock market crash of 1929, home sales slowed and many people lost their jobs. When banks closed in 1933, some depositors lost their savings. Of the 39 families who attended the Methodist Church at Green Haven, only one man had work. Many people who had no money and no food came for help to Steven Everd, the local magistrate. He distributed quantities of milk and flour and canned goods, but he finally told county officials that he could not feed all the people who were hungry. He offered the county the use of his former dry goods store, and social workers distributed food and used clothing there.

Annie Kess, a black midwife who lived near Lipin's Corner, offered maternal and child health care monthly at her home, because black families in the community had no place to go for medical care. When women who worked on Gibson Island told

The community honored Raymond Benton, Pasadena mail carrier for 41 years, when he retired in 1961.

The Schramm Collection

A 1954 reenactment of delivering mail in Pasadena by sleigh.

The Schramm Collection

Margaret, George, and Vivian Schmidt packing strawberries on the Schmidt farm about 1933. The farm was at the present site of Lake Shore Plaza.

Photo: Marion Warren

William L. Cook packing Long John cantaloupes while Urma and Margaret Benson pack tomatoes, 1939.

Photo: A. Aubrey Bodine in *News American* Collection of Jacques Kelly

Racing car built by James Billingslea Calvert in 1937.

Collection of James B. Calvert

Charles Calvert with his 1932 dark blue Ford roadster with cream wheels. The car had side curtains and a well on each side for a spare wheel.

Collection of Charles Calvert

their employers about their need, Mrs. Curt P. Richter and her friends, working with people in the community, sought permission to use Judge Everd's empty store on Mountain Road and enlisted Dr. William J. French, the County Health Officer, to organize a community health unit there in 1938. This was the beginning of the Magothy Health Center where Annie Kess served for decades. In 1953 the *Afro-American* newspaper named her to their Honor Roll for her "unusual and outstanding record." In 39 years of service to residents of the Pasadena peninsula, she delivered 1,500 healthy babies.

Though farming had been the lifeblood of the Pasadena peninsula for 150 years, the thirties were a difficult time for farmers. They always had received their highest prices for the first of each crop because customers waited all year for garden-fresh peas, beans, tomatoes, and fruit. During the thirties, refrigerated trucks from the Carolinas and

Georgia brought fruits and vegetables to the Baltimore market before those crops ripened here. Local farmers then received lower prices for their produce. After planting, cultivating, harvesting, and marketing crops, a farmer might have a loss instead of a profit. Some farm families found other sources of income. George Schmidt, whose farm extended from Hog Neck Road to the present Lake Shore Plaza, advertised hauling stone, sand, gravel, and wood; later, he owned a hardware store. William L. Cook continued to farm, but his wife, Urma Ilene Williams Cook, owned and operated a dairy with delivery routes on Gibson Island and Pinehurst.

But all was not doom and gloom during the Depression. For 25 cents each, a family could go to a waterfront resort with a picnic lunch, claim a table shaded by trees, and spend the day on the wide beach. Families discovered inexpensive pleasures like softball games between Pinehurst and Milbur, a

Emma Jenkins and friends at a family picnic at Rock Hill, now called Wishing Rock.

Collection of Emma Jenkins Wade Sanders

regular Sunday event at the boys' camp. Most communities supported Boy and Girl Scout programs. Strawberry festivals, crab feasts, and oyster roasts added zest to family life. In the winter, men hunted quail and ducks, while young people enjoyed skating parties on Cook's Pond near the end of Mountain Road or on Oakley's Pond on Pasadena Road. Judge Everd's daughter, Mildred Oakie, recalls that "during the depression, neighbors all pulled together. That was all you had—each other." And that was enough.

Churches and schools remained the centers of community activity. Families looked forward to Sunday School picnics and church suppers held on the Cook's wide beach. A new church founded at Pasadena in 1934 as the J. Selby George Memorial Church still exists today, though it has been called the Pasadena Assembly of God since 1938. Parents on the peninsula were known for their faithful support of their schools. During the thirties and early forties, Jacobsville School won the P.T.A. banner for the best attendance in the county every month for eleven years, impressive evidence of parental loyalty.

Emma Schramm (center) and brothers Louis and William, 1933.

Photo: A. Aubrey Bodine, in *The Sun*
The Schramm Collection

Ice skating at Cook's Pond, 1937. The pond is now within the community of Milburn.

Collection of James Calvert

Pupils at Jacobsville
Elementary School in 1937.

Collection of Henry A. Schmidt

Recess time *(top)* and the
Safety Patrol *(right)* at
Pasadena School in 1937.

Collection of Herb Sappington

Riviera Beach Volunteer Fire Company's fire fighting equipment in 1935.

Collection of Riviera Beach Vol. Fire Co.

The community also supported the Riviera Beach Fire Company. Founded in 1931 with Mac Eisenbach as the fire chief, the company stored its first engine in a garage behind Eisenbach's general store. They built a firehouse in 1935 and bought an ambulance in 1937. This marked the beginning of the longest continuous ambulance service in Anne Arundel County. The Ladies Auxiliary raised funds for a second engine, a second ambulance, and an enlarged firehouse. In addition to several state awards, the six-man rescue team led by Captain Edwin Raynor won an international competition in Florida in 1964, becoming the World Champion

Rescue Squad. Edwin Raynor Boulevard is named for their fire chief who died after suffering a heart attack while fighting a fire.

Active businesses on the peninsula in 1931 included S. M. Johnson and Herbert R. Linthicum, contractors; Holmes Brothers' groceries, meat, and ice at Lake Shore;

Riviera Beach Fire Company's World Champion Rescue Squad in Florida *(left)* and receiving a commendation in the Anne Arundel County Courthouse *(below)* in 1964.

Collection of Gladys Rowens

Louis Schramm, Jr., with flowers that made the Schramms the chief gladiola growers in the eastern United States.

The Schramm Collection

Charles Williams' store on Mountain Road; Frank Simmons' meats, groceries, and fruits on Tick Neck Road; A.B. Drummond's groceries, meats, and confectionary at Boulevard Park; A. Reinhardt's groceries, meats, and provisions at Greenland Beach; and C.H. McCullough's butter and eggs delivered by auto. At Pasadena, V. Vogel, C. Karcher, Leroy Williams, and Walter J. Johnson sold meats, vegetables, fruits, and groceries. In addition, the very fine sand dug from the Arundel Sand and Gravel Company's pit near the Pasadena railroad station was always in demand.

A local business that grew into an extensive operation began when William Schramm (son of Louis) built a greenhouse and began to raise flowers as a hobby. In 1933 he sold his flowers at Cross Street Market on Saturdays and on the Baltimore-Annapolis Road on Sundays. His success led the family to devote entire fields to floriculture. By 1933 he and his brother Peter were in business as florists. Soon they were planting 700,000 gladiola bulbs for successive blooms throughout the season and cutting as many as 8,000 stems in a day, making them one of the largest gladiola farms in the eastern United States. They also raised a variety of potted plants in greenhouses to supply two stalls in Cross Street Market. When drought threatened their flowers, the Schramm brothers dammed a stream and built an extensive irrigation system.

Other new businesses prospered despite the Depression. At the end of Lake Drive at Bayside Beach, Henry F. Stroback bought six boats to rent in 1932. He built more row

The Schramm farm in 1936: *(top)* irrigating rows of dahlias; *(below)* Louis Schramm, Sr., and sons Peter and William cutting gladiolas.

The Schramm Collection

Stein's Store on Mountain Road at East Shore Road. Rosalea Della serves a customer while *(below)* a 1932 Oldsmobile awaits. The store later became Della's.

Collection of Rosalea Della

Walter Phelps's Gulf gas station on Mountain Road in 1938.

Collection of Clifford Phelps

boats, and opened a small store in 1936 where he sold staples and canned goods to neighbors and oystermen. In addition, he captained three forty-foot fishing boats. In 1938 Marie Angel Durner and her husband, Marvin Durner, became the owners of Angel's grocery store. During the same year, Stein's store on Mountain Road at East Shore Road opened and Walter Phelps began to sell Gulf gasoline at his filling station nearby on Mountain Road.

The Community Methodist Church at Riviera Beach was open only from Memorial Day until Labor Day during the thirties. James Jenkins, who owned a farm on Tick Neck, offered to donate land for a church that would be open all year. After meeting in a home in Riviera Beach to make plans, in 1931 the group built Jenkins Memorial, an independent church that was open to all. Charles Harrison, the founding pastor, served there until his death in 1954.

Langley Field football team en route to play at Loyola College. Fog forced their plane to land near Heintzman's on Fort Smallwood Road on October 13, 1933.

Photo: *News American*
Collection of Jacques Kelly

The county completed Fort Smallwood Road in 1932; electricity arrived the same year. Elections were held then in the polling house on Mountain Road between Catherine Avenue and Armiger Drive. Few cars used Mountain Road, and people sat on their front porches and entertained themselves by identifying the cars and loaded farm trucks that passed. For several decades, William T. Jenkins was in charge of maintaining all county roads in the Third District. He had a crew of only six men, but that was enough. When he died in 1959, the county commissioners passed a resolution recognizing his conscientious and devoted service.

Unusual entertainment came to the peninsula in September of 1936 and 1937 when the James Adams Floating Theater docked at Green Haven. This show boat inspired Edna Ferber to write a popular novel, *So Big*. The boat itself was a barge 128 feet long and 34 feet wide, and the shows were plays performed before appreciative audiences on coastal waterways.

James Adams Floating Theater that docked at Green Haven in 1936 and 1937.

Collection of Jack Mellin

Show Boat, the famous Floating Theater, aboard which Edna Ferber made many trips, before she was inspired to write "Show Boat," is now moving lazily over the Chesapeake Bay, and will dock at the Wellwood Country and Yacht Club wharf, North East River, for a special

Ice packed against the shore at Bayside Beach on March 1, 1934.

Collection of James B. Calvert

During the late thirties, the Stony Creek Whippet Club offered another diversion, a dog racing track on Fort Smallwood Road. The managers printed a schedule of races with the names of whippets entered in each race, and the Riviera Beach Fire Company Auxiliary provided food to raise funds. However, church members who opposed gambling associated with dog racing called for a referendum vote that ended whippet racing in the early forties.

The terrible hurricane of August 23, 1933 was a long-remembered catastrophe. The water level was so high that a house floated across Gray's Creek and beached on the opposite shore. At Bayside Beach, the water lifted a bungalow on the creek side of Southwest Road and floated it across land to Harbor Road. Bob Meyers was able to take a boat from the Patapsco across land to Boyd's Pond. During the night of the hurricane, Thomas Steinhise, the lighthouse keeper at Seven Foot Knoll, risked his life by going out in an open launch to rescue the crew of a sinking tug. At Pinehurst, the storm destroyed the bath house, wrecked the pier, toppled trees in the picnic grove, and flooded the parking lot with four feet of water.

A second catastrophe involved the loss of lives. About 7:20 p.m. on July 27, 1937, flames suddenly engulfed the steamboat *City of Baltimore* on its way to Norfolk. The captain directed the ship toward Bodkin Point, but it hit a sandbank and stuck there. The ninety passengers and the crew were forced to jump overboard to escape the intense heat. A nearby freighter and other ships sent lifeboats to the rescue, and small craft from the shore joined the effort. Boats brought some of the passengers to Bayside Beach where residents cared for them until ambulances took them to Baltimore. By midnight the ship was a shell. Two people were known dead and two were missing. The following

House that floated across Gray's Creek during the 1933 hurricane.

Photo: *The Sun*
Collection of Howard Belford

day residents of Pinehurst and Bayside Beach watched as three Navy seaplanes searched for bodies near Seven Foot Knoll.

Throughout the thirties, Raymond Benton continued to carry mail to all the residents of the Pasadena peninsula. Edward Seipp became a rural carrier in 1940. Two years later, he entered military service for the duration of the war. When he came home, he and Benton divided the route, Seipp serving the area from Lipin's Corner to Hillman's Corner (now Pastore's) and Benton covering the remainder. Edward Seipp was appointed acting postmaster in 1947 and served as postmaster from 1948 until his retirement in 1972.

During the thirties and forties, many young people from Baltimore spent weeks on

Girl Scouts at Camp Whippoorwill: *(above)* saluting the flag at Captain Robinson's former home; *(right)* a Campfire Circle and dramatics beside the Magothy.

Top: Girl Scouts of Central Maryland
Right: Collection of Jack Kelbaugh

the Magothy at summer camps where facilities continually expanded. Grachur bought adjoining property, built cabins and a craft house, and sponsored a camp for underprivileged boys. Camp Whippoorwill added an infirmary and a lodge and built the Big House after the old Robinson home burned in 1939. During the summers of 1934 and 1935, Senior Scouts Mary Alice Douty and Margaret McClellan carved a totem pole that told the story of camp activities, creating a familiar landmark on a bluff above the Magothy.

Men on the peninsula could join the Magnolia Democratic Club that had its own clubhouse in Green Haven before 1939 or the Stoney Creek Democratic Club that has been a power in Anne Arundel County politics since 1938. The largest Democratic club in the state, Stoney Creek has 700 members who still meet weekly in their large club-

house on Fort Smallwood Road. Women have been full members since World War II. Residents of Riviera Beach organized Riviera Beach Improvement Association during the

Edward Seipp on the Pasadena school bus he drove in 1935 and 1936.
Collection of Edward Seipp

Green Haven Improvement
Association Carnival, 1934.
Collection of Mildred Everd Oakie

First Boy Scout troop in Pasadena with
their scoutmaster, Slater Bryant, in 1938.
Collection of Herb Sappington

late thirties. In a nearby community, men formed the Powhatan Beach Fire Company in 1940. Edward M. Dunn, Sr., a founder, served as Fire Chief for forty years and was elected to the Fireman's Hall of Fame.

Family activities in the 1930s included the Jacobsville P.T.A. amateur show, a turkey dinner hosted by the Magothy's Men's Bible Class, a card and game party for the benefit of the Magothy Health Center, a motion picture show at the Magothy Church hall, the Riviera Beach Fire Company Auxiliary's sour beef and roast pork supper, and the Magothy Girl Scout and Brownie Pack's tour of Green Spring Dairy with their leader, Mary Calvert.

Business was slow for the Rock Creek Steamship line by 1940. In 1936 the Effords had bought the *Mohawk* and had built a new pier at Fairview to accommodate this large steamer. But in 1939 the first dual highway in Maryland (Governor Ritchie Highway) made travel to beaches by car quick and easy. When war began in Europe, fuel was scarce for steamers that did not carry freight. The Rock Creek line sold their steamboats and suspended operations in 1941. An era ended when the Maryland Yacht Club bought Fairview in 1945. The Club built slips and piers on Wall Cove and made the old Fairview Hotel into their clubhouse.

Maryland Yacht Club formerly the site of
the Fairview Hotel and amusement park.
Photo: Marion Warren

Bob Lawn and Rosella Raker in a baby carriage when they were neighbors in Green Haven in 1944. They celebrated their 35th wedding anniversary in 1998.

Collection of Bob and Rosella Lawn

With war clouds threatening, activities on the peninsula continued: Nathan Stinchcomb took the Mt. Carmel Boy Scout troop to Skyline Drive, the minstrel show at Magothy Hall featured Warner's stars from WCBM Radio Theater of the Air in Baltimore, the Riviera Beach community organized a Girl Scout troop in 1941 and a Boy Scout troop in 1942, the Woman's Democratic Club raffled a quilt, and the Waterman's Protective Association planned a card party at Long Point. At Pasadena, the Third District Democratic Club and the P.T.A. sponsored card parties. But the realities of war were about to replace parties and dances. Charles Calvert was among the first to be called into service in the U. S. Army. Sixty-two of the young men who had spent carefree days at Camp Grachur saw action in Europe or the Pacific.

Life changed for everyone when the United States entered World War II. This was a time of total dedication to the war effort through military service, employment at defense plants, and support of gas, tire, meat, sugar, and shoe rationing. Our allies and our own country desperately needed tools of war and ships to deliver them. Unemployment had been the worry of the thirties; finding enough people to fill defense contracts was the challenge of the forties.

Families looking for work at Maryland Drydock, Bethlehem Steel, and other defense contractors arrived on the Pasadena peninsula from Virginia, West Virginia, the Carolinas, and Tennessee. They often came with no more than they could carry in an old Ford and moved into former summer cottages where they discovered the wonders of electricity and indoor plumbing. Boats took workmen to defense plants across the Patapsco daily. At the Pasadena Yacht Yard, one can see a flight of steps that once led to a pier where men boarded boats for Sparrow's Point.

Sparrows Point, a short distance across the Patapsco River from Fort Smallwood Park.

Photo: Marion Warren

These newcomers were assimilated into the community as their predecessors had been because they were hard-working, honest, friendly, church-going people. Virginia Moore, principal at Riviera Beach during the forties, visited the homes of her pupils and recalls that all the parents were good people who were concerned about their children. She feels that negative descriptions of the newcomers are unfair; those families were used to a simpler life far from a large city.

The war seemed close when a single-engine training plane plunged into the Magothy River off Swan Cove in September of 1943. An Army lieutenant and a private died when the plane sank in eighteen feet of water. Police, firemen, and residents pulled the wrecked plane ashore and recovered the bodies of the pilot and co-pilot.

One business that prospered during the war was William Chairs' Lake Shore Bus Company. With the gas shortage, people depended on a bus line that sent station wagons to pick up customers who lived off the regular route. During the war, the Lake Shore Bus Company served twenty communities and transported more than one thousand workers daily to defense plants.

On a breezy Easter Monday in 1944, a fire near the Magothy burned 200 acres, threatening the communities of Sillery Bay, Gray's Creek, North Shore, and Boulevard Park. Five hundred people fought the blaze for five hours. Despite the efforts of nine volunteer fire departments, Coast Guard units, soldiers from Fort Meade, and a large battalion of prisoners of war, the fire burned six dwellings, four garages, a barn, three boats, and several automobiles. At Sillery Bay, flames completely surrounded the Earleigh Heights Fire Company for two hours. Residents of encircled homes at Boulevard Park had to escape by boat. The Red Cross set up an emergency station with hot coffee and sand-

Fatal crash of an Army plane near Swan Cove in 1943.

Photo: *News American*
Collection of Howard Belford

Red Cross workers at the Holmes Pavilion serving coffee to firemen who fought the terrible fire on Easter Monday, 1944.

Collection of John Williams

wiches for firemen who remained on duty through the night. (Years later Jane Pumphrey Nes attended a dinner party in Salzburg, Austria, and discovered that the white-haired gentleman next to her had been in command of the prisoners of war who fought the fire near her childhood home.)

A direct result of the fire was the founding of the Lake Shore Fire Company in 1945 with Thomas Holmes as president. The organizational meetings were held in Holmes' store, and the group soon bought a second-hand fire engine that they kept in a barn. Since the old White Marsh Methodist Protestant Church had been abandoned after the branches of the Methodist Church united in 1939, the auxiliary raised money from dances, raffles, card parties, and an oyster roast to buy that property and build a fire house. Firemen held a carnival that raised $1,000 for a new engine. By March of 1946,

with William Harrington as fire chief, they began 24-hour service.

World War II ended at last in 1945. To honor the local men who gave their lives for their country, a veteran's memorial was dedicated beside the Green Haven Fire Department. Once more, the peninsula faced a post-war rush to the suburbs, but this time people had cars and a road system that made daily commuting to the city easy.

Members of the Lake Shore Fire Company in 1945 and (below) their first truck.

Collection of John Williams

Rapid Growth: A

Slippery Slope

The post-war rush to the peninsula began as soon as veterans returned, and it has not stopped. Peace, prosperity, a growing population, good cars, and good roads encouraged home buyers to move to the country. The population of the Pasadena peninsula more than doubled in the decade after World War II. Where else could veterans live that would be near work in the city and near the beautiful waterfront that had been their childhood playground? Because lack of labor and low prices had affected farming, many property owners were willing to sell their land to developers. The stage was set for growth at a pace ahead of government planning, and the struggle to balance the owner's right to develop his land with the stability of the environment was about to begin.

Development had stopped during the war when gas was rationed and building materials were scarce. Now property sales resumed at a frantic pace. Robert Christian worked with his father to open new sections in Green Haven. They bought a Willys Jeep and adapted it to remove the stumps of trees that they felled to make room for homes. Then Robert put logs together to make a drag and laid out streets to 15th Street. His wife Marie remembers friendly neighbors and the young people's A T and L (All Tired and Lazy) Club

Postcard showing Green Haven and Joy Harbor.

Collection of Jack Kelbaugh

that planned parties and dances. She also recalls a Sunday afternoon when the only two cars on Outing Avenue ran into each other.

Rapidly growing Green Haven organized a fire department in 1947 with Milton Behm as the first president. In 1949 the company built their first fire house and bought an old fire truck. The Ladies Auxiliary sponsored various activities to raise funds for the purchase of a pumper in 1952 and an ambulance in 1956. Members of the community formed the Green Haven Improvement Association in 1955, while the High Point Improvement Association began in 1952.

As the population grew, more churches ministered to families on the peninsula. The Chelsea Community Church began with Sunday School classes in the Magothy Beach community hall in 1948. Supporters raised funds to build a church there in 1950. Faith United Methodist Church evolved from an early Sunday School and community church in Green Haven. Worshippers organized formally as Green Haven Methodist Church in 1949. A Lutheran congregation built a church west of Stony Creek in 1945. In 1946 Father Raymond Kelly became the first priest

assigned to St. Jane Frances Roman Catholic Church in Riviera Beach.

Children from a wide area attended the overcrowded Jacobsville School until the Riviera Beach Elementary School opened in 1944. During the next two years, the Board of Education built a one-story brick school with eight classrooms at High Point and added a third room to Magothy School for black children. In 1949 the Board built the first junior high school on the Pasadena peninsula at Green Haven and named it for George Fox, who served as Superintendent of Schools from 1916 until 1946 and replaced 80 small schools with 54 modern buildings.

George Fox Junior High School, the first junior high on the Peninsula, built in 1947.

Photo: Blue Moon Aerial Photography

(Previous page) Waterside path at Downs Park.
Photo: Marion Warren

Growth was evident everywhere on the peninsula. D.C. Strain built homes at Lake Shore and developed Lyndale nearby. Many communities like Venice on the Bay, North Shore, and Rockwood Beach began with a few summer homes before the war. In the post-war years, more families built permanent homes there. These were neighborly places where people knew and helped each other. Beginning with three beach houses in 1942, the Rockwood neighborhood now includes 86 homes. This is typical of the growth of many local communities.

Long before most people were conscious of the importance of the environment, Charles Pumphrey organized and became the first president of the Magothy River Association in 1946. In June of 1947, a group of men formed the Stoney Creek Fishing and Hunting Club. Their purpose is to encourage and stimulate interest in fishing, boating, and hunting and to engage actively in conservation of fish, game, and other natural resources.

Several service clubs began in the forties. George Schmidt, along with Al Corey and Fred Kaatz, launched a recruitment drive that led to Charter Night at the Lake Shore Rotary Club on January 28, 1948. The club met at Mt. Carmel Church with Fred Kaatz as the first president. In a short time, members organized a Boy Scout troop, expanded the Magothy Health Center, and raised money for community service projects. During the fifties, they maintained a loan chest at the Health Center where people could borrow crutches, walkers, or wheelchairs. Also in 1948, Edward Seipp became the first president of the Pasadena Rotary Club that met at the Pasadena Methodist Church. At Riviera Beach, residents organized a Lions Club in 1949.

CORN-FED — Henry Schmidt and Bill Stammer with one of the corn-fed hogs that will be slaughtered for the Lake Shore Rotary Club's "Big Pig Jig," to be held at Mount Carmel Church Hall, Mountain rd., this Saturday from 7 a.m. to 5 p.m. Fresh pork sausage meat, as well as fresh hams, shoulders, chops and other cut of fresh pork will be on sale. Price of the meal is $1.25, and proceeds are for the benefit of the club's community service projects.

Henry Schmidt and Bill Stammer advertising the Lake Shore Rotary Club's "Big Pig Jig."

Newspaper clipping.
Collection of Henry Schmidt

After Dr. Breit retired in 1948, Dr. Randall McLaughlin took over his practice. Dr. Brady Smith in Riviera Beach and elderly Dr. Gaalas on Bodkin Neck were the only other medical doctors between Glen Burnie and Annapolis. Dr. McLaughlin, a stranger to the area, made daily house calls. To save time when he answered an emergency call, he identified the nearest point that he could find and asked the caller to meet him there. Though he had regular office hours in his home, he was available to anyone who knocked on his door at any hour of the day or night.

Robert Bottomley, who had retired from farming, real estate, and other business interests, sponsored contests in the schools to encourage children to develop skills. He gave prizes to the boy who built the best birdhouse and the girl whose sewing was judged best. During the 1940s, he visited Jacobsville School annually and showed the children some of the 3,000 Native American artifacts that he had collected locally.

Among the truck farmers who adapted to changing times were the Schramms. In 1946 William and Louis Schramm (grandsons of Louis) began to raise turkeys. Schramm's Turkey Farm started with 5,000 birds. Eventually they sold 12,000 dressed turkeys each year. In 1948 they opened a roadside stand on Mountain Road and combined raising turkeys with growing vegetables, fruit, and flowers for retail sale. Emma Schramm (who had taught at Jacobsville and High Point schools since 1948) and her cousin Evelyn Schramm joined them as partners in 1965.

Alfred and Walter Klingelhoefer and other local farmers adapted to post-war conditions by planting tobacco and selling it in the field instead of cutting, stripping, curing, and marketing an unfamiliar crop. Walter Klingelhoefer was the only Anne Arundel County farmer who planted 51 acres in asparagus. He added a platform to the front of a jeep to transport asparagus from the field to a packing shed where it was trimmed and tied in bunches. This venture was successful.

Another post-war venture had unforeseen results. Though slot machines were legal only in Nevada and Southern Maryland, Anne Arundel County issued eleven licenses to slot machine distributors, including three on the Pasadena peninsula. By the late 1940s, pinball machines, console slot machines, and "one-arm bandits" were everywhere—at beach resorts, restaurants, drug stores, and even grocery stores. When the machines produced large profits, the license holders began to exert considerable influence on county officials.

Schramm's Turkey Farm.
The Schramm Collection

Schramm's roadside stand
on Mountain Road.

The Schramm Collection

Dusting the tobacco crop, 1950.

Raising tobacco on the
Klingelhoefer farm.

Collection of Dolores Klingelhoefer

Tobacco planter with water tank . Four men
setting plants, four rows at a time, in 1947.

THE WALTER KLINGELHOEFER FARM IN THE EARLY 1940s

Collection of Dolores Klingelhoefer

The family farmhouse

Asparagus packing shed as seen from the house. The house was located near the present intersection of Mountain Road and Maryland Route 100.

Walter Klingelheofer and his John Deere tractor.

Raising a tobacco barn.

Sawmill ready to saw a log.

Gable's Store on Mountain Road at Brookville Road in 1947.

Photo: William L. Gable, Jr.

As population grew, commercial ventures on the Pasadena peninsula prospered. By 1947 Florence Gable had opened Gables' grocery store on the corner of Mountain and Brookville roads. A 1947 brochure lists forty-four advertisers including the Riviera Beach Pharmacy, Wirth's New Modern Fountain, restaurants, a bakery, a florist, two beauty parlors, two barbers, and two hardware stores. Customers needing electrical work or plumbing and heating could patronize D.C. Strain and Son or Fred Kaatz's Electrical Service at Lake Shore. Easter's Pavilion on Long Point sold electrical appliances as well as seafood and beer, and Daubert's Marine Railway not only rented boat slips and repaired motors but was also a restaurant and tavern.

At Riviera Beach in 1942 Elizabeth Frisino transformed an old farmhouse that had belonged to the Thomas family into a resort hotel called "Locust Lodge." Louis S. Doetsch, one of the young veterans who came to the Pasadena peninsula in 1945, founded the Pasadena Yacht Yard when the surrounding land was all woods. It survives today. Bill Stallings opened a Betholine station at Mountain Road and Disney Avenue in 1947. Later he added hardware, and the business became Dunlap and Stallings hardware store.

When Fran Koslowski and her husband, Robert Dickson, opened Tall Oaks Restaurant in 1949, her neighbors were Sanders Park, Pat and Bill's Tavern, and the old Colonial Beach Hotel. Tall Oaks had been Reamer's grocery store, but she and her husband removed two of the interior walls the day they bought it. They had six tables and 24 chairs when their restaurant and grocery store opened. In 1952 110 seats were added. Tall Oaks survives and prospers as a popular restaurant today.

The Williams' 20'×20' store on Fort Smallwood Road west of Stony Creek in 1948. This business later became the Fort Smallwood IGA store.

Collection of Clinton Gosnell

Tall Oaks 50th anniversary celebration.

Photo: Blue Moon Aerial Photography

Tri-fold advertisement for Wilson's Garage—front *(left)* and inside.

Collection of Henry Schmidt

Old farmhouse at Riviera Beach, converted into Locust Lodge resort hotel in 1942.

Collection of Dolores Rocklin

Notice for charity Bull Roast at Kurtz's Beach, April 23, 1950.

Collection of John Mason

BULL ROAST

MOOSE MEAT—
Delbert Beane, Governor of Baltimore Lodge No. 70, Loyal Order of Moose, and Mrs. Myrtle Durham, have a preview of 1,700 pounds of Steer, to be served at Kurtz's Shore at Paradise Beach on the Bay, on Sunday, April 23, 1950, at the Charity Bull Roast. The principal items on the Menu: 100 Halves Beer, 250 lbs. Hot Dogs, 700 Loaves of Bread, 3000 Hot Dog Rolls, 500 Bunches of Spring Onions, 500 Bunches of Radishes, and all the Ox Tail Soup You Can Eat.

Bring all the kiddies and make a day of it. Oh Yes, we haven't forgot the Kiddies as there will be all the soft drinks they can drink, so make it a day's picnic.

Busses leave Moose Home. 410 West Fayette Street, every half hour.

Entrance to Bob Meyer's Pasadena Beach.

Collection of Bob and Hope Meyer

Instead of arriving at beach resorts by steamer, people came by car to old favorites or to new places like Sunset, Pasadena, and Belhaven beaches. Family-owned resorts close to the mouth of the Patapsco were the Milburn family's Alpine, Carolyn Meyer's Knoll View, Robert Meyer's Pasadena, the Grantlin family's Maryland Beach, and Kurtz's Beach. On Saturdays churches from Baltimore, Laurel, or Towson brought busloads of people for Sunday School picnics. Often a hundred buses would create a traffic jam as they returned home along narrow country roads.

The Rev. Hiram Smith, a Baptist pastor, opened a new resort called Beachwood in 1948. Despite the usual restrictive covenants, he became the first black man to own land on the upper Magothy when he bought acreage adjoining a small resort called Beachwood Forest. With the help of his children, he cut trees, cleared the land, and advertised their creation as Maryland's finest interracial beach and amusement park. His advertisement shocked the community and resulted in attacks in newspapers, many

mean-spirited acts, and a lawsuit. While the lawsuit was pending, the Supreme Court ruled in 1948 that states could not enforce restrictive covenants against black ownership.

Many black churches hired buses to take their members to Beachwood for recreation and for religious services. People anchored their boats in the Magothy to watch Rev. Hiram Smith lead a line of white-robed candidates for baptism into the water. Among the attractions at Beachwood were picnicking, boating, crabbing, fishing, and a small amusement park. Three motor launches

Kurtz's Beach and their
parking lot in June 1946.

Collections *(clockwise from top)*:
Jack Mellin, Jack Kelbaugh, John Mason

took passengers down the Magothy as far as the totem pole at Camp Whippoorwill. Across the road from Beachwood was a black Girl Scout camp called Whispering Pines.

Though many beach resorts closed during the fifties, hundreds of cars and buses filled Beachwood's two parking lots. Corporate groups like Black and Decker and Westinghouse arranged picnics for their black employees there because it was the only place the white managers could go with them.

Visits from World Champion heavyweight boxers, Joe Louis and Jersey Joe Walcott, were memorable occasions. After buying Beachwood Forest and adjoining land, Rev. Hiram Smith owned eighty acres on the Magothy. He sold lots to two black doctors from Washington and then to a local black man, Franklin Owens. Beachwood closed in the early sixties when access to the ocean, private pools, and alternative amusements made local resorts obsolete.

Half of Anne Arundel County was farmland in 1948, and much of the Pasadena peninsula was still rural. Dr. Randall McLaughlin recalls a farming community then, "before the onslaught of housing developments and mini-malls." Many families came to the area only in summer, and old residents knew all the permanent residents. During the next two decades, trees were felled, roads were widened, and crossroads became shopping centers. The county commissioner form of government was not able to solve problems caused by uncontrolled growth. Without zoning laws, development was haphazard, and citizens' groups called in vain for an adequate water supply, proper sewage disposal, and long-range planning.

Life on the Pasadena peninsula was not only affected by problems of local government; the federal government called upon this region to participate during the Cold War of the fifties, just as it had done during earlier wars. Fear of Soviet long-range bombers led the U.S. Army's Antiaircraft Command to plan a line of defense around Baltimore that included a large station on Robert Bottomley's farm on Fort Smallwood Road. The gun batteries in place there in 1952 were later converted to Nike missile batteries. The Fort Smallwood Nike station was deactivated

Farms, housing, and mini-malls co-exist, but the Schramm farm remains an island in the midst of development.
Photo: Blue Moon Aerial Photography

in December of 1962 because the Russians were no longer relying on manned bombers.

The Baltimore and Annapolis Railroad ended passenger service in 1950, marking the triumph of the gasoline engine over the railroad and the steamer, but new and old organizations were active. Milton Norris and Murray Sheetenhelm founded the Mountain Road Kiwanis Club on December 24, 1952; the same year, the Lake Shore Democratic Club was organized with women as full participants. Also in 1952, the 191 members of the Grachur Club celebrated Labor Day on Cockey Creek with sailing, canoe races, softball, volley ball, and ping pong tournaments.

Other changes occurred in the mid and late fifties. In 1954 Sherman Bouyer, John Coats, George Caldwell, Sr., and the Rev. Charles Pearman (grandfather of Judge Clayton Greene) organized the Freetown Improvement Association. The Bodkin Yacht Club on Main Creek operated in 1957 from a marina, but in 1962 members bought and remodeled a former tavern to use as their clubhouse. The Pasadena Post Office advanced to first class in 1958, and Riviera Beach became the first area to qualify for door-to-door mail delivery in 1959.

Both old and new churches were active at this time. On May 23, 1954, the St. Andrews Episcopal Church congregation began to worship on Tick Neck Road. Also in 1954, members of Magothy Methodist Church created an outdoor chapel with a stone pulpit under the tall trees behind their church. Their next project was a modern education building. Pasadena Methodist Church bought property on Ritchie Highway in 1956, welcomed their first full-time pastor in 1957, consecrated their new brick church in 1958, and broke ground for a Fellowship Hall in 1962. The Lake Shore Baptist Church began in 1958 as a mission of Grace Baptist Church at Sunset Beach. A year after becoming an independent church in 1963, they moved to their present building. At Pasadena, the Assembly of God made a major addition to their church in 1961.

Vacation Bible School at the Pasasdena Assembly of God about 1955.

Collection of Herb Sappington

Few changes had been made at Magothy School for black children when the Supreme Court decision on integration led to closing the school in the mid-1950s. At that time, children still carried drinking water there in buckets and used outside toilets. The county built new schools to serve the growing communities of Lake Shore in 1953 and Pasadena and Riviera Beach in 1955. Lake Shore was remodeled in 1958, and Freetown welcomed a new school in 1959.

Drive-ins, where people could eat food in their cars, were new in the 1950s. Young people especially enjoyed this novelty. Brookwood Farms (where Mountain Road now leaves the Ritchie Highway) was the first to sell ice cream and milk shakes to lucky young men who had a car and a date. Another Brookwood Farms store soon opened on Fort Smallwood Road opposite the present Community Methodist Church. In the 1960s, it became Lee's Drive-In.

Other changes in the business community included a modern Esso station that replaced the old Klug's store in 1954, a barber shop, expanded bus service, and the sale of Angel's store. In 1956, Lewis Frazetti opened a barber shop with two chairs at Riviera Beach. This shop has six chairs today, but it no longer offers one dollar haircuts. By 1956 the Chairs bus line owned ten buses that made fifteen round trips to Baltimore daily. William Chairs sold the Lake Shore line to the Baltimore and Annapolis Railroad Company in 1960; the Mass Transportation Administration took over the route in 1973. In 1959 Marvin and Marie Angel Durner sold Angel's store to Andrew Goodwin. Plans to change its name were abandoned when customers insisted that the store was Angel's.

Many beach resorts were having financial problems in the fifties. When the Bay Bridge opened in 1952, people could reach the ocean in a few hours. Others had their own

Brookwood Farms Drive-In,
a popular place in the 1950s.
Collection of Jack Kelbaugh

The former Maryland Beach Hotel adjacent to Kurtz's Beach now is a private residence.

Photo: Marion Warren

the Bodkin peninsula for their radio transmission equipment, used for ship-to-shore calls. They also acquired and maintained a cemetery where local residents who died between 1822 and 1872 are buried. With new technology for ship-to-shore calls today, the telephone company no longer needs the transmission tower and the future of this small but historic cemetery is in doubt.

During the 1950s, while population grew by 75 percent, the county commissioners struggled to handle resulting problems without adequate zoning or long-range planning. Citizens groups responded by working to replace government by county commissioners with charter government. Businessmen on the peninsula recall that getting permits to build or expand during the fifties was difficult without "passing money." At the same

pools, free of the new worry about water pollution. Families had a choice of many diversions, and a trip to the beach was no longer anticipated with excitement. Marginal businesses began to depend on slot machine revenue, and slot machine owners held notes or liens on many local taverns and resorts.

In 1955 the Chesapeake and Potomac Telephone Company bought three acres on

Angel's Store in 1959 when Andrew Goodwin bought it from Marvin and Marie Angel Durner.

Collection of Anne Matson

Mr. Goodwin in the store in 1961.

Collection of Joyce Clocker

time, slot machine owners were taking more than ten or fifteen million dollars a year from the county's economy without providing products or services. They also were spending large sums to support local candidates for public offices.

A proposal for a referendum on legalized gambling divided the community in 1961. *The Sun* and many churches supported the proposal, insisting that the tremendous influence of the eleven slot machine license holders over elected officials retarded the county's economic growth. Owners and patrons of the many businesses that depended on revenue from slot machines circulated petitions against the referendum. On March 2, 1961, all taverns on the Pasadena peninsula and elsewhere in the county closed from six until ten p.m., and slot machine owners provided 32 buses to take people to the State

House to oppose the referendum. The proposal for a referendum failed, amid *The Sun's* charges of attempted bribery of elected officials.

On the positive side, during the next year John Henry (Harry) Hancock's will provided that the old stone house called *Hancock's Resolution* and ten acres of surrounding land were to be given to an appropriate historical society. Built about 1783, this one and one-half-story native sandstone house with a gambrel roof is a rare example of an 18th century stone dwelling. Since Harry Hancock and his sister, Mary Adeline (Mamie), lived in their family home all their lives without modernizing it in any way, the house and grounds offered an ideal opportunity for study and use as an historical site. In 1964 the Historic Annapolis Foundation took title to the property.

Hancock's Resolution about 1965. A gray seven-passenger 1915 Paige touring car with red wheels is parked nearby.
Collection of Charles Calvert

Galilee Lutheran Church, built in 1964. The round sanctuary was added in 1992.

Photo: Blue Moon Aerial Photography

Jacobsville Elementary School, 1963–1998.

Photo: Blue Moon Aerial Photography

New schools, new churches, and the opening of Maryland Route 100 brought changes to the peninsula. The Jacobsville School that replaced the 1926 building in 1963 was located across and farther down Mountain Road than the old school. Northeast Senior High became the first senior high to serve the Pasadena peninsula. Members of the Galilee Lutheran Church met in Lake Shore Elementary School before they built their church on Mountain Road in 1964. In 1992 they added a large sanctuary to their building. The Chesapeake Christian Center Church of God on Tick Neck Road began as the Pasadena Church of God in 1963. Today

they emphasize a strong youth ministry. In 1964 Route 100 cut like a knife slash across the peninsula and enabled traffic to move quickly toward the end of Mountain Road. Eventually it led to further congestion.

Despite tremendous growth, the Pasadena community remained neighborly. When Al Klingelhoefer was injured seriously in a car accident in 1965, his friends in the Lake Shore Rotary Club knew that he was concerned about his tobacco crop. They cultivated the young plants, and the Riviera Beach Fire Company used their pumper to fill the tank on his planter to water the tobacco. When it flowered, his friends sold the crop in

Internal Revenue Service agent destroying 39 slot machines confiscated in a raid in June 1966.

Photo: *New American*
Collection of Jacques Kelly

the field. After his death, his family leased the farm for use as a riding stable, and horses were stabled in a converted tobacco barn.

People awaited the results of the 1964 election eagerly because they were voting on an issue of lasting importance. Voters endorsed the proposed charter, replacing the county commissioners and providing for long-range planning and a merit system. Also in 1964, the state legislature voted to abolish legalized gambling. Both votes resulted in changes that affected the peninsula.

Memories of the 1960s are as varied as the people who are remembering. Growing up near the Magothy Bridge, one resident recalls catching rockfish that were two or three feet long and selling a dozen freshly-caught crabs to neighbors for a dollar. Teenagers gathered at Frank and Regina's where pool tables were an attraction, and families drove to Severna Park to patronize Read's Drug Store or the Safeway before Lauer's Super Thrift opened. For her, these were the good old days. A visitor who returned to Rock Creek in 1966 found his former peaceful anchorage filled by piers. Around Wall Cove, instead of forests where wildlife roamed, he saw a shipyard and many buildings. To him, the changes were tragic.

Aware of the need to conserve open space, Anne Arundel County purchased Lake Waterford Park in 1965 and opened it to the public in 1966. Located at the intersection of Pasadena Road and Waterford Road (route 648), this land had been the site of the old Magothy Mill and successive water-powered grist mills. The 68-acre tract included a twelve-acre lake. When the Maryland Historical Trust reviewed the property, they identified a fieldstone mill foundation and other artifacts. The county has developed the site, stocking the lake with catfish, bluegill, bass, and trout and providing tennis and basketball courts, ball fields, and picnic areas.

Richard Shoemaker on the Magothy in the boat he built and named *Cranky*, 1966.

Collection of Debbie Shoemaker Smigovsky

(Facing page) Lake Waterford before dam was built in 1991.

Photo: Blue Moon Aerial Photography

Pastore's Italian Grocery Store, formerly Hillman's Store from 1911 to 1968.
Collection of Anne Matson

Changes in old businesses occurred during the sixties. After the death of John Wilson, Senior, his son John managed Wilson's service station. He remodeled the building and added space for inspection and repairs. Wilson's has provided first jobs for many local young people, including Norman Huffman who started to work there at the age of sixteen and never left. After 1971 Andrew Goodwin's daughter and son-in-law, Joyce and Tom Clocker, owned Angel's store.

In 1968 Les Rizzo bought the old Hillman's store on Mountain Road at Hog Neck Road and began to operate it as Pastore's Italian Grocery. Les and Marge Rizzo and their two employees stocked shelves with many types of olives, seventeen kinds of cheeses, rigatoni, manicotti, and linguine, as well as lasagne and spaghetti. They had to teach their local customers how to prepare these foods, but Italian families came to Pastore's from as far away as Brooklyn and Annapolis. Marge Rizzo sold home-made pizza kits years before other stores carried pizza. The Rizzios treated customers like members of their family. When they brought their baby home from the hospital, they found the parking lot jammed with people waiting to see her.

In 1968 residents of the Pasadena peninsula benefitted from a result of charter government, the county's adoption of a comprehensive zoning plan. Though this plan did not stop growth, it did slow the rate of development. Haphazard expansion on the peninsula ended and ramshackle sheds and trailers disappeared. Applicants for permits to build had to attend hearings that sometimes lasted for eight hours, but now there was a fair process to follow.

Many new schools reflected the growth of population during the seventies. Bodkin and Sunset elementary schools opened in 1970 and 1971. Riviera Beach Elementary School was renovated that year, the new Magothy Middle School became the first open-space secondary school in the county in 1974, and Fort Smallwood Elementary School opened in 1977. In 1976 the Board of Education built Chesapeake Middle School and Chesapeake Senior High near the end of Mountain Road, despite community protests that the complex was too near the narrow tip of the peninsula. Its location has increased traffic problems there ever since.

Signs of progress included research at *Hancock's Resolution*, a new library, a new church, and a new road. In 1971 archaeological excavation yielded important information about *Hancock's Resolution*. When the Riviera Beach Library opened that year, it replaced a small community library on Fort Smallwood Road that had served the area since 1964. A congregation that began to worship in a rented building in 1970 built the Magothy Seventh Day Adventist Church near Magothy Beach Road in 1973. In 1979 it became the Pasadena Seventh Day Adventist Church.

The Mt. Carmel congregation renovated and reconsecrated their church in 1977. As traffic congestion became an increasing problem during the late seventies, the county built the first phase of Edwin Raynor Boulevard to connect Magothy Bridge Road and Mountain Road.

Lake Shore baseball team at Looper's Field on North Shore Road, 1971.

Collection of Dale Courville (back row, right)

Riviera Beach Public Library, opened in 1971.

Photo: Blue Moon Aerial Photography

Chesapeake Senior High School, built in 1976.

Photo: Blue Moon Aerial Photography

Water pollution was a major problem of the seventies. During the early sixties, local fishermen often caught quantities of bass and trout and three bushels of crabs a day. Older residents recall the clear blue-green waters of the creeks and rivers years ago when they could see oysters on the bottom of the river through eight feet of water and when vacationers washed their sheets in the Magothy. Because people were not aware of damage to the environment, boats flushed waste and boaters dumped beer bottles and other trash into the water. Even more serious was industrial waste that polluted the creeks, the Patapsco, and the Chesapeake Bay. When pollution killed underwater vegetation, the wide white sand beaches eroded.

The seventies also brought positive changes to the Pasadena peninsula. John Mason, president of Kurtz's Beach, Ltd., remembers only one store during the sixties, almost no one living in the area during the winter, few schools, no sidewalks, and no banks. In contrast, he says, planned development resulted in more tax dollars and better schools, sidewalks, improved roads, and businesses where residents could find a wide variety of goods and services. Furthermore, the upwardly mobile new residents of the area proved to be an asset to the community.

Residents of the peninsula benefitted when the Patapsco River Power Squadron, which had been based in Baltimore since 1916, moved to Riviera Beach in 1972. With Louis Doetsch as commander, in 1973 they rebuilt an old building there to serve as their headquarters. Originally only adults benefitted from their educational program that included teaching seamanship, piloting, and celestial navigation. Since training now is mandatory before young people can operate a boat, volunteers from the Patapsco River Power Squadron teach a basic boating course for novices under the supervision of the Department of Natural Resources. Graduates receive a certificate qualifying them to operate a boat legally.

Another group that promotes the welfare of residents of the Pasadena peninsula is the Chesapeake Woman's Club, organized and federated in 1977. They worked for a branch library in Lake Shore and serve there as volunteers. Their annual fashion show and luncheon raises funds that enable the club to support the Youth Art Fund, Save the Bay, and displaced homemakers. Recently the club received a first place award for community service in statewide competition.

In an effort to speak with a united voice, communities along Mountain Road formed the Greater Mountain Road Council in 1975. In 1980 the organization expanded to include the entire peninsula and became the Greater Pasadena Council, an umbrella association for forty neighborhoods. Representatives meet monthly to discuss civic issues.

Commercial ventures of the seventies that are thriving today include Lauer's Super Thrift and Locust Lodge. Lauer's filled a need in an area where there were few groceries in 1974. Now the two stores at Chesterfield Plaza and Riviera Plaza sell a variety of products. About 1972 Elizabeth Frisino transformed her Riviera Beach hotel into an assisted living facility for the elderly. After she retired at 85, her niece took over management of the fifteen-room Locust Lodge. A fire that destroyed Angel's store shocked the community in 1977, but Tom and Joyce Clocker soon rebuilt. Since then, they have enlarged Angel's twice.

In 1977 Anne Arundel County acquired more than 200 acres on the Chesapeake Bay adjacent to Pinehurst for use as a county park. Owned in colonial times by Charles Carroll of Carrollton, this land was rented and farmed by Augustus Schmidt from 1887 until 1913. Then a Baltimorean, H.R. Mayo Thom, bought the property as a summer

Riviera Beach's first McDonalds with a "backwards drive-in." Car's passenger side faced the service window!

Collection of Barbara Houck

Lauer's grocery store at Riviera Beach, opened in 1972.

Collection of Tom Redmond

Former resort hotel, Locust Lodge, now adapted for assisted living.

Photo: Blue Moon Aerial Photography

home and enlarged the farmhouse to twenty rooms. His family's many guests enjoyed the formal Victorian garden, a gazebo, a bathhouse on the waterfront, and seven summer cottages for family and friends. Later these cottages were rented to summer vacationers. Thousands of people now enjoy this property as Downs Park.

Downs Park opened to the public in July of 1982. There local residents could take advantage of many recreational opportunities or enjoy the natural beauty of 231 acres on the Chesapeake Bay. Visitors of all ages could spend their time picnicking, fishing, hiking, and biking. Active sports included tennis, basketball, handball, softball, and volleyball. A children's play area, a trail for joggers and bicyclists, and a nature trail offered a choice of activity. Others could seek one of the Bay overlooks or the restored Victorian-style Mother's Garden for quiet contemplation.. In addition, patrons could rent pavilions, hire the Chesapeake Room for meetings, or view the collection of artifacts and photographs that Rick Holt, Park Superintendent, has assembled.

The Thom family's home at Rock Beach Farm from 1913 to 1937, the present site of Downs Park.

DOWNS PARK

The "gang" that played at Rocky Beach Farm.

Peg Giddings and the Thom girls at Rocky Beach Farm.

All photos:
Collection of Downs Park,
Rick Holt, Superintendent

Good news came from the peninsula's oldest park at Lake Waterford. In 1984 a $400,000 building program provided four tennis courts, two baseball fields, improved trails, and picnic pavilions. Deborah Yeater became the first full-time superintendent in 1987. In 1988 the community planned a playground there to be financed and built by volunteers. Designed by children from High Point, Pasadena, and Folger McKinsey schools and funded in part through the children's "Pennies from Heaven" drive, the playground was the beneficiary of dances, raffles, and contributions from fraternal organizations and businesses. Eighteen months of planning ended in five days of intensive construction when an open field became a playground, a dream achieved through the efforts of a community known for support of its children.

Growth continued to bring changes. Magothy Bridge was rebuilt in 1980, a third lane was added to crowded Mountain Road about 1983, and the county completed Edwin Raynor Boulevard north of Mountain Road in 1985. With the population center moving eastward, in 1986 the Pasadena post office on Ritchie Highway closed, and an enlarged post office at Lake Shore became the main post office with Riviera Beach its only branch. People who live in old Pasadena now mail packages at Severna Park. In 1989 the Pasadena post office at Lake Shore celebrated its 75th birthday with exhibits, displays of old and new mail vehicles, guided tours, and a presentation by Emma Schramm who wrote a comprehensive history of the post office in 1985.

As further evidence of growth, Our Lady of the Chesapeake became the second Roman Catholic Church on the peninsula when the congregation built a church across from Bodkin School in 1983. They had met at the school when they were a mission of St. Jane Francis Church in Riviera Beach. Today they are planning to build a parish hall. In Pasadena, members of the Gethsemane Church of God in Christ had been holding services in the home of their founding pastor, Dr. Raymond Showell, since 1982. In 1985 the congregation moved to the building on Chestnut Street that originally had been the Pasadena Methodist Church.

In 1985 a tragic fire destroyed the century-old Bodkin schoolhouse, a building of architectural and historical significance that had been built by Jefferson Cook and moved to the grounds of Mt. Carmel Methodist Church. Two years later, fire destroyed the Bodkin Yacht Club on Main Creek. Members' efforts to raise funds were so successful that they were able to rebuild just eighteen months later. Other significant changes were the renovation of the aging George Fox Middle School in 1989 and the merger of the Green Haven and Powhatan Beach Fire Companies to form the Armiger Fire Company on Mountain Road at Solley Road in 1990.

Miss Fire Prevention Float
in Little League Parade.

Photo: Blue Moon Aerial Photography

Poplar Ridge.
Photo: Marion Warren

Though the business community had expanded, owners of the many successful businesses on the peninsula had no way to discuss common interests and no unified voice. That situation ended when Edward Lauer founded the Pasadena Business Association and became its first president in 1986. The group held bimonthly meetings, published a newsletter, communicated with legislators, funded scholarships, and planned annual social events. The PBA has increased steadily in size and service to the community.

From two employees in 1968, Pastore's had grown until Les and Marge Rizzo employed sixty people in 1984 when they asked Bryan Metzbower to be their partner. They demolished their original building in 1987 to make room for a larger store that was part of a small mall. In September of 1991, Bryan and Sue Metzbower became the owners of Pastore's Italian grocery and deli. An equally old landmark, Klug's grocery store and filling station, was replaced in 1989 by a modern convenience store and Texaco station.

After four years of negotiation, in 1989 Anne Arundel County signed a 25-year agreement for the development of *Hancock's Resolution* near Bodkin Point as an historic park under the supervision of the Department of Recreation and Parks. Historic Annapolis Foundation, Incorporated still holds title to the property, The County Executive, James Lighthizer, provided $150,000 in the county budget in 1989 for hiring a consultant to draw plans for restoration and taking steps toward development of the site.

The Pasadena peninsula faced the last decade of the twentieth century with much to cherish from its past—friendly people, community spirit, natural beauty of the waterfront, and easy commuting to the city. But problems related to rapid expansion remained as residential communities continued to replace what had been productive farms.

Sailing by moonlight
at Pinehurst.

Collection of Jack Mellin

The Threshold of the

Third Millenium

As the decade of the nineties began, the big problems facing residents of the Pasadena peninsula were traffic congestion and water pollution. Two-mile backups occurred when commuters tried to reach their homes from the point where route 100 merged into Mountain Road. People who lived below Lake Shore Plaza had to allow ten minutes to wait for a break in traffic that would permit them to enter Mountain Road during commuting hours. Despite these problems, families were grateful for better schools, better housing for all, more doctors, a wide choice of goods and services, and more business and career opportunities. Of the 51,356 people living on the Pasadena peninsula in 1990, only 11.6 per cent engaged in farming or construction; 19.8 per cent were in trade and 25.1 per cent were providing services.

Water pollution remained a concern, especially for once-beautiful Rock Creek that formerly attracted thousands of excursionists every summer weekend. Now a foul odor came from its murky waters. Headlines in *The Sun* and the *Maryland Gazette* in 1989 and 1990 announced "Rock Creek Tributaries to Stay Closed for Another Year," and "Troubled Tributary Focus of Clean-up." Community leaders complained that the county's sewage pumping station at the head of Rock Creek was back-flushing sewage into the creek.

Fishing at Bayside Beach on the Patapsco.
Photo: Blue Moon Aerial Photography

Newspaper headlines from January through July of 1992 continued the story: "Compromise May Save Rock Creek Plan," "Fate of Rock Creek Hangs in Balance," "Army Corps of Engineers Rejects Dredging Plan," "Rock Creek Gets $300,000 State Funds for Dredging," "Dredging Begins," and, at last, "Dredging Removes Odors from Rock Creek." Behind these headlines is the story of a community's struggle to save a priceless asset. Since the installation of an aerator that pumps oxygen into the water, there has been no fish kill and no contamination of the creek.

News from the Magothy was encouraging. By the late 1980s, recreational fishermen were reporting improved fishing in the river and the Chesapeake Bay. The Magothy had been closed to fishing for yellow perch since September of 1983. In April of 1992, yellow perch returned after ten years' absence, and there was hope for a reinvigorated Magothy. As a result of federal legislation, industrial waste was no longer as serious a threat to the Patapsco River and the Chesapeake Bay as it had been formerly. In another area, a plan to level wetlands at Bodkin Point in 1993 angered residents who successfully opposed damage to a critical area.

At Lake Waterford, the embankment was leaking and silt was seeping into the lake. In 1991 an old pipe collapsed and flooding followed. Despite community concern about preservation of the foundation of an old mill, replacing the 1925 dam meant the loss of that site. While building the new dam, workmen found nails that were dated to the 1600s. The foundation stones from the old mill have been saved to make an historical marker. Recently botanists have found growing at Lake Waterford the only two known Maryland specimens of a rare variety of box huckleberry.

Anne Arundel County planned another green space on the peninsula in 1991 when it acquired 157 acres of the former Klingelhoefer farm on Fort Smallwood Road for a public golf course. It was to be named in memory of James A. Moore, a local fireman who lost his life fighting a forest fire at Yellowstone National Park. This project is scheduled for completion in 2001.

Steps taken toward restoration of *Hancock's Resolution* at this time included reinforcing the floors, reshingling the roof, repointing the mortar, and painting the trim. When William Mason gave the county the 19th century Cook farmhouse, the county moved it to *Hancock's Resolution* and renovated it to serve as the home of the caretaker. The home where Rhoda Hancock lived after marrying Henry A. Cook in 1887 had returned to the site of her childhood home.

A decade-long struggle for a library in Lake Shore ended in 1994. The Chesapeake Woman's Club circulated a petition and collected 4,500 signatures, proving to officials that many people who lived in that area wanted a library. With the support of local Councilman Carl (Dutch) Holland, the County Council approved an appropriation to renovate four storefronts in the Long Point Mall to make space for the new library. The 90,000-square-foot Mountain Road Branch Library cost 1.6 million dollars and opened with 55,000 volumes and eight librarians.

(Previous page) Lake Waterford.
Photo: Tom Redmond

Home of Henry Alfred Cook and Rhoda Virginia Hancock Cook, now moved to the grounds of *Hancock's Resolution.*

Collection of James B. Calvert

Lake Waterford.

Photo: Marion Warren

A native of Pasadena, Renee Neisser Shanahan, became the only person in the history of the Miss Universe Pageants to hold all three state titles and to compete in all three nationally televised beauty contests. In 1987 Renee Neisser won the title of Miss Maryland Teen; in 1992 she became Miss Maryland; and in 1995 Renee Shanahan was named Mrs. Maryland. Her husband, David Shanahan, held the titles of Mr. Maryland Teen in 1985 and Mr. Maryland in 1987, making the Shanahans the only couple ever to have held both sets of titles. Another local resident was honored when the Lake Shore Volunteer Fire Company dedicated its new

Renee Neisser Shanahan as Miss Maryland, with Governor Schaefer in 1992.

Collection of Helen Neisser

Lake Shore Volunteer Mobile Rehab Unit in the 1998 Pasadena Parade.

Photo: Kathy Vanik, *Maryland Gazette*

William G. Rothamel, 53-year veteran of Lake Shore Volunteer Fire Company, and Chief Elbert Cordle at the dedication of the new pumper-tanker in 1997.

Collection of Howard Belford
Photo: *Maryland Gazette*

Cyclone II Pumper-Tanker to William G. Rothamel, a volunteer with the company for 53 years.

Residents of the peninsula were willing to spend time, effort, and money to fight zoning, development, and environmental battles whenever they believed that their communities were threatened. Controversy over expansion of a marina in 1997 led one community to file suit to oppose boat racks that were prohibited by a covenant. Public hearings were well-attended and discussion was heated. A proposal to close Woods Road to through traffic was quashed by activists who feared that the change would result in increased traffic congestion on Mountain Road. Strongly differing opinions about widening Mountain Road versus creating a bypass led to meetings where tempers flared when hundreds of people packed schools and community halls. In each case, controversy reflected residents' sincere concern about the future of their community.

The Pasadena peninsula is still attracting new residents in great numbers. In 1981 the Chesterfield neighborhood consisted of fifteen homes; in 1999, over 5,000 people live in 1,576 homes there. The average price of a single-family home on the peninsula was $146,135 in 1995. Young people who had grown up on the peninsula wanted their families to live there.

Though the Schramms were reluctant to part with most of their grandfather's farm, overwhelming estate taxes forced their decision to sell 180 acres to Koch Homes. When development began in 1989, headlines in *The Sun* announced, "Old Turkey Farm Lays Golden Egg." Bordered by Mountain Road, Catherine Avenue, and routes 100 and 648, many homes in Farmington Village, a community of 448 single-family homes and townhouses, have been selling to people who live nearby. The Pasadena Business Association's new office building is on the site of the Schramm's old roadside stand.

In December of 1997, the Anne Arundel County Council considered a countywide proposal prompted by severe congestion on Mountain Road during commuting hours. Residents of waterfront communities urged officials to monitor traffic impact and stop development on "jammed" roads that were the only access route along a peninsula. Existing laws had proved to be ineffective. The county executive, John Gary, proposed that a relief road be constructed on the narrow tip of the Pasadena peninsula. Discussion of this alternative or widening Mountain Road continues.

When many residents and their representatives realized that development would occur as long as land was available, they proposed reserving undeveloped land as green space. Delegate Joan Cadden lobbied for this concept and felt encouraged when Maryland's Board of Public Works approved $155,525 in open space money to buy 14.85 acres adjacent to the Lake Shore Athletic Complex. This property will be used for park facilities, linking the Athletic Complex to Jacobsville Park, and will be designated as part of the Magothy River Greenway.

Old businesses on the peninsula continue to prosper. In 1998 Angel's store celebrated its 75th anniversary and the retirement of Rosie O'Connell, who had served patrons for 38 years. At the age of 83, she recalled many customers who had shared their joys and their troubles with her. Now a second generation of the Clocker family, Walter and Andrew, manage the store. In addition to the Schramm farm, which has undergone major changes, and Angel's and Pastore's (formerly Hillman's), which have changed ownership, only two businesses survive from the 1930s. They are Wilson's service station, opened in 1934, moved to its present site in 1937, and owned by the son of the founder, and Kurtz's Beach, established in 1933, owned by Bonnie

Pasadena peninsula's recent history illustrated: a remnant of the Schramm farm adjoining new homes on former farm land.

Photo: Marion Warren

Wedding party of Cindy Walker and Perry Crandall in Kurtz's gazebo.

Photo: Martin Sheehan

and Gus Kurtz, and operated by Kurtz's Beach, Ltd. (Bonnie Kurtz and her cousin, John Mason). Kurtz's now specializes in wedding receptions and other catered affairs.

The two oldest churches on the peninsula, Magothy and Mt. Zion United Methodist Church, remain active. Mount Zion, founded in 1859, renovated their building in 1998. The congregation's multi-year fund raising effort made possible construction of a new fellowship hall, offices, kitchen facilities, and improvements to the sanctuary. The $750,000 project ended with a a dedication and consecration service. Mt. Zion's annual week-long Magothy Camp Meeting attracts thousands of worshipers from Baltimore and Maryland counties.

Changes came at two schools in 1998 and 1999. In April of 1998, teachers, students, and the entire community held a farewell party for the Jacobsville School that was built in 1963. Games, face-painting, and a silent auction occupied children and adults who crowded the halls to say goodbye and to express their appreciation of the old school. That summer it was demolished and replaced by a new school with improved technology and without portable classrooms. When children returned to Riviera Beach Elementary School in the fall of 1999, they found the building thoroughly renovated and they at last had walls instead of open space classrooms. This project was the result of years of parents' efforts to secure funding.

(Center) Magothy Methodist Church, across Mountain Road from the original 1794 log church.

Collection of A. A. Co. Division of Planning

(Bottom) Historic Mount Zion Church, renovated and enlarged in 1998.

Photo: Jon Armentrout

Monument to area veterans placed by World War II veteran Samuel G. Kemp on Mountain Road at Route 100. Community groups and individuals contribute to the periodic replacement of the American Flag.

Photos: Jon Armentrout

The modern Jacobsville School, built in 1998.
Photo: Marion Warren

Residents of the Lake Shore area who were tired of taking their children to Baltimore for indoor soccer games formed the Lake Shore Limited Partnership and designed a seven million dollar indoor sports arena that includes plans for three 200- by 85-foot air-conditioned rinks, an ice skating rink, a soccer rink, and a multi-purpose rink. A glass mezzanine for spectators, a pro shop, and two meeting rooms complete the design. The Partnership, with Jim Renner as general partner, signed a thirty-year agreement to lease land from the county at the Lake Shore Athletic Complex. They have received zoning approval to build near the intersection of Route 100 and Mountain Road and expect to break ground in the fall of 1999. One goal of the project is to sponsor wheelchair hockey games and Special Olympic soccer programs for the disabled.

A new organization called Friends of Hancock's Resolution has been working on developing the educational potential of that site since 1997. They authorized an historical evaluation of the house that year, while The Lost Towns of Anne Arundel Project conducted a study of the eleven surrounding acres. When Anne Arundel County allotted $150,000 for preservation and restoration of *Hancock's Resolution* in 1998, the state agreed to match that contribution. The county also added twelve and a half adjacent acres to the property. The 116 members of the Friends of Hancock's Resolution, with James R. Morrison as president, envision the property as an educational experience for viewers who will visit the restored buildings, enjoy living demonstrations, and see the store stocked to show its relationship with the oyster fleet.

Despite a one-year moratorium on building on Mountain Road, the second ban in three years, development continues in 1999. Though the area has reached the critical point, new subdivisions are approved, despite the adequate facilities law that requires enough infrastructure to support new building. Carolyn Roeding, president of the Greater Pasadena Council, has called the adequate facilities law a joke because developers can evade it by securing waivers.

Debate continues about whether to widen Mountain Road or build a bypass. Many property owners believe that widening the road would ruin their businesses. In the summer of 1999, the state added reversible turning lanes as a temporary solution to traffic jams at commuting hours. At the same time, the County Council voted to extend the moratorium on new subdivisions along Mountain Road. Pasadena's County Council representative, Shipley Murphy, sponsored the bill that continued the moratorium but permitted family subdivisions.

Lake Waterford Park.
Photo: Marion Warren

Downs Park.
Photo: Marion Warren

Mr. Pumpkin welcomes customers to the colorful display of produce at Schramm's roadside stand.

The Schramm Collection

Despite congested traffic in some areas, there are many green spaces on the Pasadena peninsula. Lake Waterford Park, Downs Park, Baltimore's Fort Smallwood Park, and the Lake Shore Athletic complex are the largest, but smaller county-owned parks like Freetown, Highpoint, Havenwood, Jacobsville, Poplar Ridge, Rock Creek, and Sunset provide space for competitive sports and other activities. Tar Cove Park is the site of the future county golf course, and *Hancock's Resolution* will be the first educational park on the peninsula. Downs Park offers varied opportunities for visitors, including a 1.8-mile Senior Exercise Trail, a Self-Guided Nature Trail, the Rocky Beach Farm Youth Group Camping Area, and the popular Bay Concert Series presented each Sunday evening from Memorial Day through September.

Sports activities for youth include the Riviera Beach Little League team, the Riviera Beach Girls Softball League, the Lake Shore Youth Baseball team, and Pasadena Chargers Football team that practices and plays at Lake Waterford Park. Doubtless there are others. In addition, local schools provide opportunities to play soccer, softball, basketball, field hockey, lacrosse, and football. Many elementary schools sponsor scout troops as well.

Boating remains a favored recreation for individuals and organized groups. The Maryland Yacht Club, the oldest club in the area, was founded in Baltimore in 1908 and moved to Rock Creek in 1945. Bodkin Yacht Club cherishes its history since 1957. Members of the Ventnor Yacht Club have dispersed to other clubs, but the Patapsco Club, dating to the forties, and the White Rocks Yacht Club, founded in the 1960s, remain active. The Magothy Sailing Association, a consortium of sailing clubs, and the Patapskut Sailing Association sponsor sailing

races and other activities on the Magothy. Membership in these clubs is by invitation.

Though agriculture had been the foundation of life on the Pasadena peninsula from the beginning until recent decades, in the late 1990s only three farms produce any quantity of fruits or vegetables. Gordon Wirth, the Schramms, and Holt's Produce are the survivors. (Cindy Ellison Holt and Rick Holt own the former Ellison farm near the end of Mountain Road.) All depend on retail sales at roadside stands or farmers' markets.

Successful businesses on the peninsula now are beyond counting. The Pasadena Business Association organized to give business owners a unified voice, but it has done more than that. From its founding, the group has raised funds for scholarships. Beginning in 1992, they have sponsored an annual Legislative Day in Annapolis where they meet with their representatives and discuss issues

Lake Shore baseball team at the complex on Woods Road, 1998.

Collection of Dale Courville, Manager (back row, right)

Annual Lake Shore Little League parade.

Photo: Blue Moon Aerial Photography

Little League—before the game.

Photo: Jim Anderson

Matt Gunther explaining the fine
points to James Anderson at bat.

Photos: Jim Anderson

Little League—after the game.

Photo: Jim Anderson

The 1971 Pasadena Chargers football team evolved from the Greater Pasadena
Touchdown Club, founded in 1968 by Kenneth Bohn, Sr., and Loren Van Brackel.

Photo: Jeanne Bohn

Cheerleaders for the Pasadena Chargers, 1971. The
Chargers play home games at Lake Waterford Park.

Photo: Jeanne Bohn

Bodkin Yacht Club.

Photo: Marion Warren

Sailing race on the Magothy River under threatening skies.

Photos: Walter Kramme

PASADENA BUSINESS ASSOCIATION

(Above) Dedication of new PBA office building in
1998. *(Right)* Annual crab feast at Kurtz's Beach.
(Below) Celebration of the Association's tenth
anniversary in 1996.

of interest to the community. Beginning in 1993, the PBA has sponsored an annual Trade Show to showcase their businesses to each other and to the public and, in 1995, the annual Pasadena Parade began. Throughout the year, the PBA gives support to community causes. The association, with Carol Cross as Executive Secretary, now numbers 280 members. Serving an area that had been fragmented by loyalties to local neighborhoods, the Pasadena Business Association has stimulated a unified community spirit. They promote the entire peninsula.

Today shoppers can buy almost anything they want or find almost any service they need at Chesterfield Plaza, Lake Shore Plaza, Pine Grove Village, Pastore's Plaza, Lauer's Riviera Beach Festival, or Long Point Mall. Gone are the days of traveling to Baltimore for medical procedures or dental care. Dry cleaners, florists, hairdressers, banks, and libraries are nearby.

Churches and schools always have been central to life on the Pasadena peninsula. Today many denominations are represented: Assembly of God, Baptist, Roman Catholic, Lutheran, Episcopal, Methodist, Church of God, Seventh Day Adventist, and the independent Jenkins Memorial, all with active programs for adults, youth, and children. Though people elsewhere often are critical of public education, on the peninsula parents are the schools' faithful supporters. Parent-Teacher Associations are active at all Pasadena schools. Neighborhoods are unified by common loyalties to schools and other community organizations.

The Magothy Health Center is still a lay health center, owned and operated by the community. Though the Health Department provides the professional staff, volunteers run a thrift shop to raise money to maintain the building and grounds. Since the founding of the Magothy Health Center in 1938, additions and renovations have been made to the building and services have been expanded, but support from the community and benefits to the community have been constant.

Growth of the area remains a problem, with hope for the future resting on adoption

Magothy Health Center, organized locally in 1938 and still operated by the community.

Photo: Marion Warren

PASADENA PARADE, 1998

Kiddie cars
on the Agro
Motors float.
Photo: Mike Agro, Jr.

GableSigns float.
Photo: Kathy Vanik,
Maryland Gazette

The Prudential Carruthers Realty float.
Photo: Kathy Vanik, Maryland Gazette

The Parade in motion.
Photo: Mike Agro, Jr.

A blue heron at rest and an osprey nest on a channel marker.
Photos: Blue Moon Aerial Photography

of a long-term plan, strict enforcement of the adequate facilities law, and expansion of the Magothy River Land Trust and the Magothy River Greenway. Those who remember the peninsula before World War II can share the memories of Jane Pumphrey Nes, who grew up near the Magothy River. She writes, "How could I have understood that my world would vanish? . . . to ride horseback through the woods alone, to watch from the river bank nature's eternal predawn ballet as a blue heron woke and flew slowly across the reeds . . . the honking of wild swans on cold winter nights, their elegant forms silhouetted in the moonlight . . . . We still sail the rivers, moor in the creeks . . . But it is different now. Rarely are we alone."

That tranquil world is gone forever. Despite the losses that accompany growth, residents of the peninsula look forward with hope to a new millennium. After decades of abuse, rivers and creeks are clearer, fish have returned, and some underwater vegetation is appearing, a promising sign for the future. Endangered species like the peregrine falcon and the bald eagle are reported on the peninsula. Today most adults are conscious of the importance of protecting the environment, and children are the environment's best advocates.

Despite the tremendous growth of the area, on the brink of a new millennium

people who live in the seventy neighborhoods on the Pasadena peninsula remain neighborly and family-oriented. Newcomers and successive generations of natives choose to make their homes there because of the wide variety of housing options, the natural beauty of rivers and creeks, the vocational and cultural resources of a large city nearby, good schools with supportive parents, active churches with varied programs, extracurricular activities for youth, a choice of places to shop, career opportunities, and green spaces that offer recreation or peaceful contemplation. As in the past, newcomers will feel the friendliness of local people and will join them in struggling to balance human needs with the needs of the environment that gives the peninsula its special character.

Lake Waterford.
Photo: Marion Warren

Photos: Marion Warren

". . . the wide variety of housing options, the
natural beauty of rivers and creeks . . ."

*N*o matter their party affiliation, elected officials representing the Pasadena peninsula are always besieged by constituents to halt further development of the area and relieve congestion on Mountain Road. Long-term State Senator Phil Jimeno agrees with those concerns.

"We all know the future of Pasadena and the quality of life for its residents depends on far reaching land use decisions made by the county and state governments," he said.

Pasadena residents are extremely proactive on their own behalf. In 1997, the Mountain Road Preservation Group was formed and supported by 17 community associations led by activist Jim Bilinki. Others had wrangled for years and several studies had been done on how to alleviate the back-ups on the notorious "dead-end road." This past summer, the MRPG finally saw one of the proposals adopted, a reversible lane to ease morning and evening rush hours.

With a serious look to the future, strong growth-halting initiatives were established by the Magothy River Land Greenway program. Led by State Delegate Joan Cadden and supported by the Magothy River Trust, application has been made to preserve from development one thousand acres of the Looper Property, Saybrooke Two, and the corner of Angel-Durner's property near Grey's bog. This is the first newly proposed greenway in Maryland in over 20 years.

Without this preservation, the consequences of development would affect the health of Pasadena rivers and creeks which flow directly into the Chesapeake Bay.

"It is my hope that these projects will educate citizens to realize fully the importance of preserving and maintaining large tracts of forested land and waterways that so directly impact the Chesapeake Bay," explained Delegate Cadden.

Lipin's Corner, where Mountain Road branched from Baltimore-Annapolis Boulevard, 1923.

Photo: Maryland State Roads Commission. Collection of Jacques Kelly

Sponsors

Angel's Food Market, Inc.

The Clocker Family, 4681 Mountain Road, Pasadena, MD 21122 / Ph: 410-255-6800 Fax: 410-255-3501

When Angel's Food Market first opened in 1923, Mountain Road was a country lane leading to weekend holidays at Pasadena beachfront communities. It was the place to stop for picnic supplies and cold drinks. When the Angel family sold it to Andrew Goodwin in 1959, the store had become the primary supermarket for the area. Mr. Goodwin's daughter and son-in-law, Joyce and Tom Clocker, bought the store in 1971. Their three sons, Tom, Andrew and Walt, have all managed the business and their children have begun working in the store.

Angel's is a much-loved store, but local residents are not the only shoppers. Salad lovers from all over make the trip to buy the famous cole slaw, macaroni and potato salads which are essential for every special occasion throughout the year. Now Angel's ready-to-serve meals, including Italian specialties, German sour beef and dumplings and Maryland crab soup, are earning the same reputation for quality and freshness. The homemade meals are available in individual portions as well as family-size meals.

With fresh produce, an in-store bakery, a large delicatessen, and quality meats and seafood, Angel's remains the principal supermarket for many people. The full line of beer, wine and liquor make Angel's truly a "one-stop" shopping destination.

It's also the place where neighbors meet one another and chat for a while in what many consider Pasadena's "Town Square." While quality, freshness and homemade food are priorities for the Clocker family, they all believe in this comfortable way of shopping. They say:

Angel's—where you are treated like a neighbor, not a number.

The Clocker family wishes to thank Pasadena for its many years of support.

(Back row, l-r) Andrew, Walt, Tom, Jr.
(Front row, l-r) Tomma, Joyce, Tom, Sr., Gwen

BGE

Public Affairs Office, Jeff Jefferson, 47 State Circle, Suite #403, Annapolis, MD 21401 / Ph. 410-269-5282 Fax: 410-269-5289 Web: www.bge.com

THE POWER BEHIND PASADENA

For more than 40 years, the power behind Pasadena has risen tall along the shores of the Patapsco River. The stacks of BGE's Brandon Shores and H. A. Wagner electric power plants are as much a part of the Pasadena landscape as seafood. And since the 1950s, those plants and the people behind them have provided the energy that has kept both Pasadena and Central Maryland moving, growing and improving.

Conceived in the first flush of economic and population growth after World War II, the first unit of the Herbert A. Wagner generating station began operating commercially on February 15, 1956. At the time it was the largest operating unit on BGE's system, generating enough electricity to supply 300,000 people. By 1972, Wagner's size had quadrupled to keep pace with the region's ever-growing demand for electricity.

While the economy slowed after the oil embargo of the mid-1970s, it bounced back in the 80s and 90s. To meet the new surge in demand for electricity, BGE's newest plant, Brandon Shores Unit 1, began operation in May 1984 and Unit 2 in May 1991.

Today, Brandon Shores ranks as the cleanest coal-burning plant in Maryland. Both units were built to burn low-sulfur coal, making them at the outset an environmentally sound, reliable and low-cost source of electricity. Over the years, BGE has continued to install state-of-the-art environmental control equipment to reduce plant emissions further and produce cleaner air for the region.

More than 300 employees work at the plants, and many of them live and volunteer in the area. In fact, BGE is the largest corporate philanthropic contributor in the state and is actively involved in a multitude of civic, cultural, educational, environmental and health and welfare organizations throughout Anne Arundel County.

BGE has had a long and proud association with Pasadena and is now looking ahead to the future. Maryland has joined the growing number of states that are deregulating their electric generation industry, giving customers their first opportunity to shop around for electricity. BGE and its power plants are competitively positioned for this new era of energy and are ready to meet the growing energy needs of Pasadena and of the region.

Situated on 375 acres along Pasadena's Ft. Smallwood Road, the Brandon Shores/H. A. Wagner Complex today generates enough power to meet the energy needs of 40% of the 2.6 million people living in Central Maryland.

Century 21 Volke Realty

Mark Volke, Karyn Volke, 4181 Mountain Road, Pasadena, MD 21122 / Ph: 410-437-1900 Fax: 410-437-1917 email: markvolke@realtor.com

(Left to right) Karyn Keating Volke, Mark Volke, Sharon Adams, Henry Summey, and Debby Price.

As lifelong Pasadena residents, Karyn and Mark Volke love this area where they have worked with thousands of families and businesses through Century 21 Volke Realty. Founded 11 years ago, the business has grown through referrals and repeat business from many satisfied clients.

"We started our business so people would have a homegrown Realtor who knows the community, is a part of the community and knows many of the residents," said Karyn. "All of our agents are full-time professionals living in this area, your neighbors."

Real estate is a natural outgrowth of the couple's love of people and their history of volunteerism. Mark has been a hurricane relief worker twice, served as church deacon, and held offices in various professional and community associations. His father, the Rev. Charles Volke, pastored Grace Baptist Church in Sunset Beach for 20 years. Mark graduated from Northeast High School and holds B. S. degrees in both business and marketing from Towson State University.

Karyn grew up in Pasadena and graduated from Northeast and Anne Arundel Community College. She has been involved in Laurel Acres-Whipoorwill Community Association and is a long-time school volunteer.

Mark and Karyn believe in the importance of family

and community. Along with their three daughters, April, 13, Candace, 12, and Claire, 8, they enjoy local sports and are active in church activities.

Mark and Karyn are serious about their profession and each holds a GRI (Graduate of Realtors Institute) and CRS (Certified Residential Specialist) designation. They and their agents are experts in residential sales and listings, commercial and land sales, property management, buyer brokerage, HUD and VA foreclosures. As part of Century 21, the world's largest real estate firm, the small, personalized agency still has the advantages of nationwide advertising, research and relocation resources.

"To us, real estate is a counseling job; we don't sell anything," said Karyn, explaining the conviction she and Mark have about their profession. "We help people make good buying or selling decisions. We use our education, experience and resources to provide all the information they need. We get to know people and develop a trusting relationship, a friendship with our clients. Then we let them make the decisions."

Mark and Karyn believe Century 21 Volke Realty continues to attract clients because they are committed to supporting their clients throughout the life-changing experience of buying and selling real estate.

Cheshire Crab Restaurant and Pleasure Cove Marina

Jerry Herson, 1701 Poplar Ridge Road, Pasadena, MD 21122 / Restaurant: 410-360-2220 Marina: 410-437-6600 Fax: 410-437-6127
Web: www.pleasurecovemarina.com

The Cheshire Crab Restaurant and Pleasure Cove Marina have an impressive array of dining and marina services assembled by owner Jerry Herson. His goal is to be a neighborhood business affordable to everyone.

"It is important to me that anyone can come here to eat, to store a boat, to get an engine replaced, to fuel up—whatever is needed—and know they are a welcome and important customer," says Jerry. "Our state-of-the-art travel lift can take care of the largest boat that can get down the Bodkin, but we want the runabout boater to feel that his business is appreciated, too."

The Cheshire Crab has a full-service bar separate from the restaurant. Among the 127 employees in the marina and restaurant are dozens of local teenagers and Jerry wants the atmosphere to be one where families are comfortable having them work there. "We are a neighborhood, family-oriented place," said Jerry.

The Cheshire Crab serves a wide variety of meals including seafood, steak and Italian specialties, sandwiches and, of course, steamed crabs.

"We always try to have crabs, and bring them in daily year round," said Jerry. "Our waterfront deck has become a popular crab-eating spot, especially the Sunday afternoon picnics during the summer. We even have beach volleyball."

The deck overlooks the deep, calm harbor of Pleasure Cove Marina. Heavy-duty lifts take the boats out of the water and store them on shore on covered racks, keeping the boats free of the ravages of the water and protecting the environment.

Offering full marine repairs including entire engine replacements, parts, fuel and water taxi service on the Bodkin, Pleasure Cove Marina offers patrons of the Cheshire Crab Restaurant a discount on their fuel. There is also the Ship's Store filled with sundries for boaters and supplies of bait and tackle.

Jerry Herson wants to become even more involved in the community and is planning a swimming pool and gymnasium which would be available to local high schools and offer low-cost memberships to the public. It may possibly include a day spa and other amenities.

"There are not many reasonably priced facilities like this in this area," explained Jerry. "I believe we can offer a total recreation center that everybody can use. I want Pleasure Cove and Cheshire Crab to be the place where everybody can relax and have fun."

Chilltrol, Inc.

Dick Roeder, Jr., 152 Blades Lane, Glen Burnie, MD 21060 / Ph: 410-360-2700 Fax: 410-761-6313 email: chilltrol@aol.com

With professionalism as its hallmark, Chilltrol has become recognized for its highly trained and experienced staff as they install and service heating, air conditioning and refrigeration systems. "I actively recruit only the top HVAC (heating, ventilation, air conditioning) mechanics who can meet the standards we set for our team," explains Chilltrol President Dick Roeder, Jr. "People know when they call us, we will handle any problem that may occur. We have the experience, the manpower and the equipment."

Starting in his home garage 12 years ago, Dick has built his business into a fleet of 50 vehicles and a team of 78 employees. "We cover the entire state of Maryland and the surrounding areas," said Dick. "About forty- five percent of our work is custom residential, forty-five percent is commercial and ten percent is industrial."

Chilltrol's residential experts specialize in custom-built homes. Homeowners have come to rely on Chilltrol for distinctive systems, whether repairing or replacing systems in older homes or designing systems for new custom-built homes. Courtesy and cleanliness, along with expert performance, have been cited by homeowners as the reason to call Chilltrol.

Always working toward the goal of making his company the best in its field, Dick Roeder is expanding carefully. Now reaching the largest industrial and government customers, including the U.S. Naval Academy, Coca-Cola, and Hewlett Packard, all employees take pride in building the business as part of the Chilltrol team. "We can attract the highly trained and experienced HVAC professionals based on our employee compensation and bonus plans," explains Dick. "I want everyone to share in the success of our business."

Always on call, Chilltrol has a 24-hour operator who can dispatch a mechanic immediately to handle any problems. With a computerized sheet-metal shop, a fully staffed Service Department, and as the second largest Trane dealer in this area, Chilltrol continues to be first when commercial, industrial and residential customers need HVAC installation and repair service.

Edison Electric Company, Inc.

Mike Thompson, 200 Holsum Way, Glen Burnie, MD 21060 / Ph: 410-582-9777 Fax: 410-582-9616

If anything defines the opportunities that hard work and small business provide, it is the history of Edison Electric Company, Inc. Once a stockboy working for Edison founder John "Jack" R. Raap, Mike Thompson is now the owner and president of the company and has built the business into one of the largest electrical contractors in the area.

Edison Electric began as a one-man business in Jack's Sunset Beach home garage in 1967. After moving to Mountain Road a year later, Edison grew along with the Pasadena community around it. By 1981, Jack had made Edison a prominent force in the electrical field with 20 employees, including Mike Thompson. Though the recession of the 80s slowed business, Jack never laid off a single employee.

Mike had worked his way up to foreman, then president, when tragedy struck in 1990 with CEO Jack Raap's sudden passing. His wife, Rhonda, managed the company for two years before selling it to Mike. The business remained on Mountain Road until the rapid growth of the building industry forced it to relocate to a larger facility in Glen Burnie in 1997.

Now with 40 employees, Edison Electric Company, Inc. continues serving the Pasadena community and surrounding areas. Residential jobs as small as installing an outlet or dimmer switch or as large as rewiring an entire home are done expertly by qualified electricians. "People feel comfortable calling Edison because they know us, and their families know our families," said Mike. "And we always offer free estimates on any job."

Edison Electric also received the coveted "Sub Contractor of the Year Award" for the past seven years from both Ryan Homes and NV Homes. This recognition for expertise in new construction has made Edison's future growth a certainty.

"We are hoping to open additional locations throughout Maryland which will eventually allow for employee ownership," explained Mike. Jack Raap's legacy of loyalty and success continues on through Mike Thompson and Edison Electric Company, Inc.

GableSigns, Inc.

Paul and Matt Gable, 7440 Ft. Smallwood Road, Baltimore, MD 21226 / Ph: 410-255-6400 Fax: 410-437-5336
email: solutions@gablesigns.com Web: www.gablesigns.com

For almost twenty years, GableSigns has been making its mark throughout Pasadena and surrounding areas with its attractive signs and attention-getting graphics. Visit any business, school, church, community or shopping center and chances are you'll see a Gable sign.

From modest beginnings in their parents' backyard, owners Paul and Matt Gable have grown GableSigns, Inc. into a nationally recognized company known for quality designs and craftsmanship.

Paul, GableSigns' founder and president, quickly developed a reputation for his talent by winning a trophy in a school poster contest when he was eight. His first "paying" sign project came at the age of eleven for a local snowball vendor. "The pay was $7.00 and free snowballs for the summer. What a deal!" quips Paul. While at Chesapeake High School, Paul took graphic arts courses and began making a pitch to local businesses for his signs.

Upon graduation in 1980, Paul saw an opportunity to turn his passion into a career and began making signs in his parents' garage. As this backyard enterprise grew with new clients and a few part-time employees, his brother Matt started committing his after school hours to the company, joining on full-time after graduation in 1985. "Without a doubt, Matt's knowledge of the industry, his enthusiasm and his motivation have been a driving force behind the succes of our company," Paul affirms.

Moving to a commercial building on Ft. Smallwood Road in 1986, GableSigns expanded its capabilities to include fabricated metal, plastic, electrical and neon signs. It was here the company grew steadily over the next

13 years as buildings and equipment were up-graded to meet the needs of customers and additional employees. "Because we started locally, many of our clients and employees live here in Pasadena," Matt comments. "We owe much of the credit for our company's success to them."

Today, GableSigns employs over 75 sign professionals and craftsmen, completing sign projects all over Maryland and surrounding areas. For some clients, their role has expanded to include shipping and installation all across the country. Regardless of the quantity or distance, the company stays focused on quality. Others agree as evidenced by the company's seventh consecutive design award granted by the United States Sign Council, an industry association with over 1,500 members.

This year, GableSigns moved to its newly constructed 40,000-square-foot state-of-the-art sign manufacturing facility. "The additional space and computerized sign-making equipment will enable us to provide better service, higher quality, and a nicer environment for our staff," Paul remarks.

Despite their growth and national recognition, Paul and Matt plan to keep their company firmly rooted in Pasadena. "It's a great place for our business," notes Paul. "And because it's our hometown, we take special pride in every project we do here."

J. B. Machine Parts and Supply, Inc.
and J. B. Marine

Dave Jacobs, 8029 East Shore Road, Pasadena, MD 21122 / Ph: 410-437-9995 or 888-437-9995 Fax: 410-360-1929
email: web@jbmarine-machine.com

When J.B. Machine puts in a boat lift, the goal is perfection. "We always use extra heavy duty material and we never skimp in any area," explained founder Dave Jacobs. "We would rather make a smaller profit and give our customer the best value."

"Our UP & OUT Boatlift was designed to keep that boating investment virtually maintenance free. We use thicker steel, more mounting bolts and stainless steel pulleys to create an extremely rugged boat lift."

As well as the boat lifts and lifts for personal watercraft, J.B. Machine designs and manufactures parts and machinery for all types of business applications.

"We are an industrial machine shop catering to the plastic, beverage, spice, recycling and computer industries," said Mike Jacobs, Dave's youngest son and general manager of the business. "We repair and maintain machines that enable our customers to keep their worldwide businesses running smoothly."

J.B. Machine provides well-drilling equipment to a wide area including Southern and Western Maryland, the Eastern Shore and Virginia. Breaking new ground, the company designed and manufactured a medical waste disposal system that can crush glass vials.

Even though J.B. Machine began as a full-time machine shop in 1973 in Dave's garage, he was still working at Koppers Company. Successful growth allowed him to make J.B. Machine his full-time career in 1980.

His wife, Shirley, has also been his business partner throughout the years. Two of the couple's five children have joined them. Besides Mike, whose wife Becky is the secretary for the company, another son, Jamie, runs engineering and sales activities.

Dave and Shirley recently celebrated 35 years of marriage by renewing their vows in front of dozens of family and friends at a celebration given by all their children. They plan to work less now and allow their children to manage the business.

"I am glad to see J.B. Machine is going to stay a family business," said Dave. "People will know that they are going to get professional workmanship and reliability since the same family owns the business."

In the photograph, left to right: Jamie, Mike, Dave, Shirley and Becky Jacobs

Jet Blast, Inc.

Kevin T. Kavanagh, 6800 Ft. Smallwood Road, Baltimore, MD 21226 / Ph: 410-636-0730 Fax: 410-636-0819 Web: www.jetblast.net

Jet Blast was founded by its owner, Timothy Wilson, in February of 1979. With only $5,000 in capital and rented equipment, Tim began working out of his father's Pasadena garage. Recruiting a few of his fellow Northeast High School alumni, Jet Blast's growth was strong and fast and Tim soon moved to the much larger location on Ft. Smallwood Road. Joined by his management team, Kevin Kavanagh, Ed Jefferson and Steve Jones, Jet Blast's commitment to quality and excellence made it one of the industry's "Top Professionals." Named by *Inc.* Magazine as one of the Top 500 Fastest Growing Private Companies in the United States, Jet Blast has received numerous awards and industry recognition.

Over the past two decades, Jet Blast has provided services to some of the largest industrial, municipal and utility concerns on the East Coast, providing safe employment to hundreds of Pasadena residents.

Jet Blast, Inc. has harnessed the force of water under high pressure and turned it into the most powerful cleaning tool ever known to industry. Jet Blast technicians use specialized equipment operating at pressures up to 35,000 psi (enough to cut through six inches of steel or three feet of cement.) Additonally, Jet Blast maintains a fleet of the most technically advanced vacuum equipment with enough power to pick up a 10-pound brick. More importantly, however, is Jet Blast's commitment to quality and safety to its employees. All of Jet Blast's employees receive the most current technical training and use state-of-the-art safety equipment and procedures.

A proud member of the Pasadena Business Community since 1979

Koch Homes, Inc.

Richard E. Pezzullo, Jr., Director of Sales and Marketing, 2661 Riva Road, Suite 220, Annapolis, MD 21401
Ph: 410-573-5720 Fax: 410-573-5257 Web: www.kochhomes.com

Quality homebuilding in Anne Arundel County has long been a tradition in the Koch family. It began in 1931 with Charles Koch purchasing 170 acres on the Magothy River for a private summer residence and future land development opportunity. The property was subsequently subdivided and developed into the community now known as "North Shore on the Magothy."

In 1951, Ross J. Koch started Bucher & Koch Realty Company, Inc., which focused primarily on custom building in North Shore and the surrounding Pasadena area. Over the next 25 years Ross Koch developed a reputation for exceeding industry standards for quality of construction and attention to detail. His son, Gary W. Koch, joined the firm in 1977 and Koch Homes, Inc. was founded a year later.

Koch Homes has become recognized as the premier homebuilder in Anne Arundel County as evidenced by numerous awards received for its outstanding achievements in residential development. It has been a five-time winner of the Anne Arundel County Award of Excellence, five-time winner of the

Sales & Marketing Council Award, and two-time winner of the Land & Development Council Award.

Some of the communities developed by Koch Homes in the Pasadena area include Whippoorwill Estates, Sillery Bay Forest, Chandler Point, Saybrooke by the Lake, Blue Waters Farm, Meadow Run and most recently, Farmington Village.

Farmington Village, once a large part of the 200-acre historic Schramm farm, is currently being developed by Koch Homes. Farmington Village includes a wide variety of housing from affordable townhomes to luxury single family homes. Koch's reputation for quality, combined with amenities such as club house, pool and walking paths, has made it one of the fastest selling new developments in Anne Arundel County.

Farmington Village embodies the highest levels of standards for which Koch Homes has been recognized. A focus on a sense of arrival, relationship of home to land, and the feeling of an overall planned environment has made Farmington Village another award-winning community.

Kurtz's Beach, Ltd.

John Mason/Bonnie Kurtz, 2070 Kurtz Avenue, Pasadena, MD 21122 / Ph: 410-255-1280 Fax: 410-255-2062

Most of the beaches that drew city dwellers to Pasadena have disappeared, but Kurtz's Beach has done much more than survive. It is home to a flourishing catering business, Kurtz's Beach, Ltd., hosting hundreds of celebrations throughout the year from elegant weddings to summertime picnics and crab feasts.

With blue waters in the background, many brides have opted for an outdoor wedding in the waterfront gazebo. In cooler weather, the magnificent octagonal ballroom offers spectacular views, with a second hall available for larger crowds.

Outside, Bradford pear trees border the beach, and picnic tables stand under expansive, shady pavilions surrounded by lush shrubs and plants. In any season, Kurtz's presents a relaxing and lovely alternative to traditional catering halls. Only the food outshines the location.

"We are very particular about the freshness and quality of ingredients that we use for meals," says Master Chef John Mason, president of Kurtz Beach, Ltd., and a graduate of Baltimore International Culinary College. "Everything is prepared right here under close supervision of myself, my partner, Bonnie, and a dedicated staff of prep chefs."

Kurtz's serves good, basic meals like those found in your grandmother's kitchen, according to John, but presented with a flair that makes every event an occasion. Many corporations, large and small, entrust their picnics and parties to Kurtz's which provides not only the food, but entertainment as well. That can include DJ's, bands, kiddy rides, magicians, clowns, and even jousting for guests. Smaller groups enjoy Kurtz's on Multi-Picnic Days when two or three groups save costs by sharing the facilities.

John's first cousin, Bonnie Kurtz, is vice president of Kurtz's Beach, Ltd. She and her husband, Gus Kurtz, own the Kurtz Beach property. It was Gus' father and uncle, Gustave and Sam Kurtz, who founded the beach business in 1933. It went through several transformations until Bonnie and John formed a partnership to turn the former public beach into a site for private gatherings in the early 90s.

John and Bonnie share a love of catering, and both agree that their success can be attributed to the many members of their family who gather every week to lend a hand. "You will find mothers, fathers, aunts, uncles, brothers, sisters, nephews, nieces—even grandmothers—working everywhere, assuring that everything is as perfect as possible. Even staff members are related to somebody because they bring their families to work at Kurtz's too."

With rapidly increasing popularity, Kurtz's Beach, Ltd., has been offered seemingly golden opportunities to open other sites. John and Bonnie have rejected this idea because they would lose the personal touch and the family assistance, both a large part of the appeal and success of Kurtz's Beach, Ltd.

Kurtz's Beach with employee family.

Lauer's IGA Supermarket and Bakery

Edward B. Lauer and Helen B. Lauer

Chesterfield Plaza, 8095-A Edwin Raynor Blvd., Pasadena, MD 21122 / Ph: 410-255-0070 Fax: 410-360-9574

Riviera Plaza, 8479 Ft. Smallwood Road, Riviera Beach, MD 21122 / Ph: 410-437-4800 Fax: 410-360-9609

"Friendly, Fast and Fresh,
Serving You Is What We Do Best!"

This motto sums up the core philosophy of Lauer's IGA Grocery Stores, says founder and president, Ed Lauer. "Quality and freshness throughout our stores are always top priorities," he explains. "All of our employees understand how important it is that customers get only the best."

When Ed opened his first store on Mountain Road in 1974, his years of experience with Food Fair had prepared him for the long hours and hard work demanded by the grocery business. He closely managed all areas of the store, working side by side with store personnel to develop the Lauer way.

His wife, Helen, took a critical look at the produce department and decided to manage that area herself until it met her standards. She moved on to the bakery department, arriving at 2 a.m. each morning, until it too represented the above motto. Lauer's now has one of the finest and most complete lines of breads, pies and cakes, including custom orders.

A true family business, all five of the Lauer daughters worked at the store during their high school and college years. Two chose it as their career. Bernadette Snoops designed and installed the scanning system in the store in 1981, making it the first independent supermarket in Maryland to use the then-new tech-nology. When the Riviera Beach location was purchased from Acme in 1982, daughter Babette Lauer Poyer joined the family business as did son-in-law Craig Snoops. Son-in-law Joseph Mill-sap joined the family business in January of 1991.

Lauer's has a family of employees too, many having worked in the stores 15 years or longer, including John Ferdock who celebrated his 25th year in 1999. A strong profit sharing plan and excellent benefits package engender employee loyalty and dedication to the business.

Education is dear to the heart of the Lauer family and "Lauer's Learning Ladder," a register tape redemption program open to all private and public schools, has provided thousands of dollars for a variety of educational tools. Strongly supporting the entire community, the store generously sponsors numerous sports teams and Downs Park concerts, provides food for church dinners and school functions, and gives discounts and direct donations to many worthy causes.

Now that both the Riviera Beach and Edwin Raynor Boulevard stores have been completely updated, the latest addition, Lauer's IGA Supermarket in Upper Marlboro, is bringing the Lauer brand of customer commitment to a new area.

TO SERVE YOU BETTER IN 2000

McCully-Polyniak Funeral Home, P.A.

Valerie Polyniak, 3204 Mountain Road, Pasadena, MD 21122 / Ph: 410-255-2381 Fax: 410-255-2604
Funeral Service, Pre-Planning, Cremation, Memorial Services

After 95 years of conducting funerals for over three generations in South Baltimore, Brooklyn, Pasadena and surrounding areas, McCully-Polyniak remains a family-owned, family-run business. "People have come to rely on our family, and trust our personal compassionate approach," said Valerie Polyniak, niece of Doris McCully and the late James L. McCully. Begun in South Baltimore by I. Few McCully, James' father, the family's philosophy has always been that of service, not business. "My uncle built this business on a man's word and a handshake. We consider everyone's financial situation and work with families during that intense time of bereavement."

With a degree in mortuary science including training in grief counseling, Valerie began working part-time with her aunt and uncle when she was 15. The relatively small number of funeral directors who are women include Doris McCully, also a licensed mortician, who served several terms on the State Licensing Board of Morticians. She and Valerie bring a special sensitivity at a time when it is most needed.

"I always try to meet personally with the families," said Valerie. "Between Aunt Doris and myself, we do see everyone at all three locations to express our condolences. People always ask for Aunt Doris because of friendship and loyalty developed over the years."

Valerie is president of McCully-Polyniak Funeral Homes, P.A., her Aunt Doris

is vice president, and her husband John is secretary-treasurer as well as general manager of the entire operation.

Formerly in investment brokerage, John joined the firm in 1998. The couple has two children: Scott, 16, a junior at Mt. St. Joseph High School where he is an Honors student and plays basketball; and Julie, 14, a freshman at Seton-Keough High School. A dancer since the age of 2, Julie also plays soccer and is active in the Galilee Lutheran Church Youth Group.

Valerie and John are raising their family in Pasadena, and are frequent Mountain Road travelers because of their business, community involvement and their children's activities. They keep the same hectic pace of most families today, but they never lose sight of the importance of their funeral service.

"After 28 years at our Mountain Road location, Pasadena families know they can rely on McCully-Polyniak to care for them as our friends and neighbors in their time of need," said Valerie.

"In this day of numerous corporate acquisitions, it brings us great pride to still be independently owned and operated. It is our hope to remain a family business for many years to come."

(Left to right) John, Scott, Julie, Valerie Polyniak; Doris McCully.

Pastore's Italian Deli

Brian & Sue Metzbower, 3820 Mountain Road, Pasadena, MD 21122 / Ph: 410-255-8822 Fax: 410-255-8906

Pasadena's own Little Italy has stood at the corner of Mountain and Hog Neck roads for over 30 years. Although bright and modern, Pastore's Italian Deli still has the soul of the old, aromatic shops which had pasta-filled barrels and meats and cheeses hung from the ceiling.

Now shelves of packaged domestic and imported pasta in a multitude of shapes and cuts sit beside jars and cans of various olive oils, roasted peppers, pepperoncini, tomato pastes and sauces, ceci beans, pesto sauce, Italian tuna—everything to make the simplest or most exotic of Italian dishes.

The delicatessen boasts imported prosciutto, capacola, Genoa salami, mortadella and other musically-named meats as well as fresh Italian sausage links. Complementing them are fresh provolone, parmagianna, romano, fontinella and ricotta cheeses. Fresh mozzarella rests in water next to ricotta salada, marinated mushrooms, and homemade salads including pasta florentine and Greek pasta salad.

While Pastore's is a gourmet cook's dream, it is perfect for non-cooks too. Here you can purchase ready-made meals for two to 200. Homemade delicacies from simple sauce to trays of lasagna are ready for dinner. For larger crowds, Pastore's is known for its off-site catering, delivering hot meals and large sandwich platters with condiments included.

Pizza is everybody's favorite and Pastore's popular pizza kit has three crusts, Don Pepino sauce and a 9-ounce bag of specially blended grated pizza cheeses, all ready for your oven. Or you can have hot pizza delivered to you door seven days a week. Ordering one or more pizzas entitles you to delivery of anything else, from groceries to subs to meals. You can also dine in Pastore's comfortable cafe.

Pastore's has a great bakery filled with fresh bread and rolls, turnovers and doughnuts, and chunky chocolate cookies out of the oven every few hours. Refrigerated cases hold cannoli, tiramisu, cassata and rum cakes. It's a popular shopping spot during the holidays for buying

Carry-out and delicatessen.

pizzelle makers and cappuccino and espresso pots, as well as fine Italian candies and cookies.

Begun in 1966 by Les and Marge Rizzo, Pastore's has employed hundreds of Pasadena residents including Brian Metzbower when he was a teenager. He and his wife, Sue, became partners in 1984, then took full ownership when the Rizzo's retired in 1997. The children of both couples, Michella and Tina Rizzo, Jessica, Katie and Ashley Metzbower, have all worked in the business through the years.

Now employing 90 people, Pastore's is the first choice when there's a celebration, a wake, a business meeting or any event where delicious food and quick service is most important. Pastore's serves today's faster-paced society and still retains the personality and warmth of an old-time neighborhood shop.

Pastore's owners Brian and Sue Metzbower; daughter, Katie, left.

Phelps' Package Liquors, Inc.

Clifford R. Phelps, 4447 Mountain Road, Pasadena, MD 21122 / Ph: 410-255-0151 Fax: 410-360-8530

In 1928, Walter J. Phelps and his wife Mary purchased 25 acres of ground at Mountain and Woods roads. Walter was a descendant of that same Walter Phelps who moved his family to Anne Arundel County when he purchased a 100-acre farm at South River in 1673.

Like his ancestor, Walter J. Phelps was a farmer, but was better known for producing charcoal for a variety of Baltimore industries. He had been operating his coal business from his father-in-law's farm on Mountain Road near Solley Road since 1895. He bought free standing timber in the area and employed a crew of men to cut it and construct "charcoal pits" on the property for the production of coal. He stockpiled large quantities of bagged charcoal which he transported to Baltimore by a two-horse wagon before he switched to a truck around 1918. Walter was listed in the Baltimore City Directory as owner of the Phelps Coal and Can Company as early as 1900.

Walter's son, Clifford A. Phelps, also worked in the family business of charcoal production and light farming on the family property. In 1935, Clifford A. Phelps married a Pasadena girl, Irene Brown, who helped in the family business. In 1937, Clifford A. and Irene had a son, Clifford R. Phelps. A year later, they opened a gasoline station at the corner of Mountain and Woods roads. In 1939, near the end of the era of charcoal burners in Anne Arundel County, Walter J. Phelps, the charcoal professional, passed away.

In 1947, the family's gasoline station was changed to a tavern which soon added a liquor store becoming a tavern and liquor store combination. By 1956, farming in the Pasadena area was a disappearing occupation. It ended for the Phelps family in the same way that charcoal production had ended ten years earlier.

When Clifford A. Phelps passed away in 1971, the family business was continued by Clifford R. and his mother, Irene. In 1972, a son named Clifford M. was born to Clifford R. and his wife. By 1978 the tavern business had been discontinued and the liquor store enlarged. Cliff M. started in the family business at age 9, bagging all the store's ice. He now works in the liquor store and operates the family topsoil business, screening and delivering topsoil and fill dirt by the dumptruck load to homeowners in the area.

Despite dramatic changes in occupations and in the Pasadena area, four generations of the Phelps family have continually adapted and succeeded in operating a business at the same location.

Walter J. Phelps holding Clifford R. Phelps, aged 2, at Phelps' Gasoline Station in 1939.

Redmond's Towing Service

Tom Redmond, 8224 Baltimore & Annapolis Blvd, Pasadena, MD 21122 / Ph: 410-360-000 Fax: 410-437-7432

Redmond's Towing Service has been known for providing quality service to the motoring public for the past 33 years. Begun by Tom Redmond when he was only 20 years old, the towing business has grown to include ten tow trucks, including wheel-lift and rollback trucks for specialty towing.

Professional drivers man the trucks and many are long-time employees of Redmonds such as Roosevelt McCauley who has been with the company for 26 years. Although based in Pasadena, Redmond's Towing has accounts throughout Anne Arundel County and the state of Maryland.

Tom Redmond has traced his roots back to 1675 when his ancestors first settled in Anne Arundel County. He was born in his grandmother's house on Solley Road and attended local schools.

A strong love of Pasadena turned him into a community and civic activist. He worked on legislative committees with the Maryland General Assembly for fifteen years. His commitment to the area was recognized when he was elected to represent this district on the Anne Arundel County Council.

Tom served two terms as president of the Pasadena Business Association, was president of the Towing and Recovery Professionals of Maryland, and was a two-term president of the Maryland Auto & Truck Recyclers Association.

A life member of both the Anne Arundel County Historical Society and the Sierra Club, Tom was the first life member of Friends of *Hancock's Resolution*. He has worked many years for literacy, local youth sports and environmental concerns.

Tom has seven children, Tom, Jr., Richard, Eric, Chad, Steven, Casey and William, and lives near Lake Waterford with his wife, Cathy.

(Below) Tom Redmond with one of his signs that have welcomed motorists along Route 100 to Pasadena for over 25 years. *(Right)* One of Redmond's earlier welcoming signs in 1974,

TeleRep Call Centers

Sandie and Don Olson, 14 Wellham Ave., Glen Burnie, MD 21061 / Ph: 410-761-2424 Fax: 410-761-3357 Web: www.telerep.com

When Sandie Olson decided the minimum wage she was being paid as an answering service operator was not enough, her husband, Don, a U. S. postal worker, encouraged her to start her own service. She took that challenge in 1975, beginning Arundel Telephone Secretaries, Inc. with only three small businesses that needed an answering service. As clients increased, Don joined her and they founded TeleRep Call Centers which now serves over 600 clients across the United States.

TeleRep is firmly committed to providing quality jobs for area residents. The corporate headquarters on Wellham Avenue in Glen Burnie has just been expanded to include all three floors that accommodate the almost 90 new employees who have joined the 60 already employed there.

All TeleRep operators are highly trained professionals using the latest technology. Sandie began in her basement with an old switchboard like the one used by Lily Tomlin's "Ernestine," but TeleRep now boasts the latest computerized phone systems. TeleRep's highly motivated Customer Service Representatives combined with state-of-the-art software allows TeleRep to represent businesses with maximum professionalism and integrity.

TeleRep still takes around-the-clock calls for plumbers, business reps and other service businesses, but it also fills the need for in-bound telemarketing and customer service. For example, the White House Historical Association catalog orders are all received and processed at TeleRep. Pizza Hut

Sandie Olson at TeleRep's first switchboard.

hired TeleRep to field all of their customer service calls from franchisees, while Pitney-Bowes uses TeleRep for customer service surveys.

The Internet is the next frontier for TeleRep, and Sandie and Don see exciting possibilities for their clients and their employees including televideo customer service.

Business success for Sandie and Don has helped their family grow closer. Evette is the sales manager, Amberly is the comptroller, and Heather is an employee trainer. Their son Wesley is 14, but he is already helping with the computers.

Almost family, Cynthia Blair-Smullin, a Pasadena native and company manager, has been with TeleRep for 20 years.

The Olsons attribute TeleRep's success to the dedication, loyalty and support of their associates and clients from Pasadena and surrounding areas.

The Olson family in TeleRep's computerized telephone center. *(Left to right)* Amberly, Sandie, Don, Heather, Wesley, and Evette.

The Bank of Glen Burnie

Joyce Cleveland, 8707 Ft. Smallwood Road,, Pasadena, MD 21122 / Ph: 410-437-2070 Fax: 410-437-6432
Web: www.thebankofglenburnie.com

CELEBRATING 50 YEARS OF COMMUNITY BANKING

In the late 1940s, northern Anne Arundel County was experiencing tremendous growth. A group of local businessmen, concerned that banking services were not keeping pace with this growth, banded together and chartered The Bank of Glen Burnie. Founded as a locally-owned, independent community bank, The Bank of Glen Burnie opened its doors in August 1949. Since that day, business has been conducted on a first-name basis.

Today The Bank of Glen Burnie serves the commercial and retail banking needs of area residents with offices in Pasadena, Odenton, Crownsville, Severna Park, Severn, and Ferndale, in addition to two locations in Glen Burnie. Customers benefit from a comprehensive line of banking products and services, 24-hour telephone banking and a network of 11 ATMs.

The Riviera Beach Office—which celebrated its 25th Anniversary in 1998—is one of the Bank's most active branches.

"We know the retail and commercial needs of our customers because we are part of this community," said Joyce Cleveland, Assistant Vice President and Branch Manager. "Our staff, directors, and stockholders live and work in these neighborhoods. You are going to meet us in the grocery store, at church and on the ball fields with our children. This is what community banking is all about."

The Bank of Glen Burnie's great strength and stability have been built on a commitment to personalized customer service, strong leadership and local decision-making. In the face of emerging technologies and overwhelming industry changes, these attributes have withstood the test of time.

The Bank of Glen Burnie pledges to carry on the tradition of community banking and is ready to meet the challenges of providing a new decade of service to all its valued customers, old and new.

Tom Clocker of Angel's Food Market with Joyce Cleveland, vice president of The Bank of Glen Burnie and Riviera Beach branch manager.

W. Ray Huff & Associates, Inc.

W. Ray Huff, 8349 Ritchie Highway, Pasadena, MD 21122 / Ph: 410-647-1111 Fax: 410-544-5735 Web: www.Huffinsurance.com

W. Ray Huff & Associates, Inc. is now insuring its third generation of clients, providing all types of insurance including health, life, auto and casualty.

"We do little advertising because the majority of our business is referrals from satisfied customers," said Ray Huff, founder and president of the agency. "We believe in service after the sale. We explain updated coverage for current policies, let clients know about changes, help process claims, and make sure the claims are paid."

Ray became a licensed independent agent in 1960, starting out in his home garage, then moving to Glen Burnie and eventually building his Pasadena office in 1967.

"I really like helping people," he said. "We have helped many, many small businesses over the years and I can honestly say that some of our commercial work saved businesses from failure."

An affable man, Ray's love of people brought him success not only in business but in the community, too. He was a respected member of the Maryland House of Delegates for eight years and served on the boards of many civic groups such as the YMCA.

His daughter, Nancy Huff Nicklow, a Salisbury University business graduate, has worked in the agency since she was a teenager. A licensed agent since 1994, Nancy is now office manager as well as manager of personal lines insurance.

Faith Vanskiver, agency vice president and commercial lines manager, has been with the company for 27 years. "I really enjoy the work, Ray is a great employer, and I plan to stay in the business."

All three agents agree that education about insurance is an important tool for financial stability and success. W. Ray Huff & Associates, Inc. now has a web site, www.HuffInsurance.com, which provides information on the many kinds of insurance and the various companies represented by the agency, along with general consumer advice.

"We find that people are unaware of things such as Motor Vehicle Administration rules regarding turning in tags when auto insurance is discontinued for any reason," said Ray. "We want them to have quick access to information and answers to their questions."

All W. Ray Huff & Associates, Inc. agents adhere to the philosophy embraced by Ray over the years. "We give people the facts, sell them what they need, not what we want to sell, and don't worry about commissions," explained Ray. "Then we don't forget about them. That's why we're serving the same families now: Grandparents who bought from us almost 40 years ago, their children and their grandchildren."

(Left to right) Nancy Huff Nicklow, W. Ray Huff, and Faith Vanskiver.

Patrons

Photo: Marion Warren

The Bay

Cross Auto Supply, Inc.
    Nelson Cross III & Matt Cross

Ventnor Marine Service, Inc.
    Arthur & Irma Humm

Countywide Trash Removal
    J. Ben Poe III

MARCOM Marketing & Communications
    William and Carolyn Melton

Winnie and Skip Maher— Maher's Florist,
    Formal Wear, & Limousine Service, Inc.

County National Bank
    Directors, Officers, and Employees

Pasadena Yacht Yard, Inc.
    Louis and Mary Doetsch

The Redmond's—Tom, Cathy, Tim Jr., Richard,
    Eric, Chad, Steven, Casey & William

In Memory of Melvin C. Beall
    Former President of Harms & Associates

The River

Baxter Tire & Auto (John & Rose Baxter)
Stoney Creek Automotive Parts
Bay Country Rentals
Anderson, Davis & Associates, CPA
AB Advertising Glen Burnie, MD
Wilson's Bus Service, Inc.
Pasadena Caterers

The Creek

Arthur & Irma Humm
Jay Humm
Robin & Wayne Brashears
Ben & Katherine Brashears
Chesterfield Homeowners Association, Inc.
Nelson III, Lynn & Victoria Cross
Matthew A. Cross
Nelson F. Cross Jr. & Carolyn Z. Cross
Tanya R. Baxter and Tennille L. Baxter
Marie Yonkoski
Ruth Poe
Mr. and Mrs. John B. Poe, Jr.
Thomas Poe
J. Ben Poe
Sharon Poe
Chris and Kim Poe
Christopher Jacob Poe
Allison Hunter Poe
Jeremy Marlin Poe
Jason Poe
Melissa Poe
My Friend "Duke" Poe
Frank Sr. and Linda Loane
Frank Jr., Julie, Chelsea Loane
Bill and Karen Loane
Senator Phil Jimeno 31st District
Delegate Joan Cadden 31st District
The Wade's: Rick, Sharrie, Ricky & Jason
Donald Bolander
East Anne Arundel Lions Club
Mr. & Mrs. James G. Macauley & Family
Dave & Shirley Jacobs
Jamie & Gail Jacobs & Family
Mike & Becky Jacobs & Family
Darlene & Bruce Follin & Family
Kimberly & Richard Zeh & Family
Charles & Beverley Madden

David Jacobs II & Family
Mr. John & Augusta Lipin
Edward J. Lipin, Esquire
Dr. Raymond J. Lipin
Senator Alfred J. & Irene H. Lipin
Ed & Sharon Woods & Family—Stony Creek
Bob, Carol, Tracey, Chris & Ben Douglas
James & Dayna Anderson
Emily J. Anderson
James J. Anderson, Jr.
Debby, Bob, Robert & Tracey Stancavage
Mr. & Mrs. William T. Upton, Jr.
Valyn Jade Tant
Lacy Naomi Tant
Richard E. Dobry, Sr. & Family
Charles & Elva Chisholm & Family
Compliments of the John G. Warner Family
John and Lois Harman Simpson
Heather Kaye Myers
Walter Stanley and Virginia Harman
Stephen, Ester & Stephanie Hoffman
Barbara and Jan Clark
The Ditch Family of Rock Hill Beach
Albert & Catherine Thyr
The Gonce Family
The Rotary Club of Lake Shore
Pat & Frank Calvert
Mr. & Mrs. Robert Baxter
Mary Rosso Family
The Backhaus Family
Ed and Diane Blake & Family
Gil and Pat Willey
Barbara Goodwin Millhauser—Riviera Beach
The Howard & Catherine Belford Family
Diana & John Wilson Jr.
Maureen & Mike Agro & Family
Saybrooke Property Owners Association
Marion Redmond

Debbie & Kristen Romano
Steve & Justin Waltz
George, Christa, Collin, and Courtney Athas
Councilwoman A. Shirley Murphy
Phillip, Ramona, Gregory & Monica Jimeno
Bill, Wendy & Amber Harris
Pasadena United Methodist Church
Pasadena Early Learning Center

In Memory of

Nelson F. Cross Sr. & Helen D. Cross
Karen M. Brackens
Bert & Charlie Griebel
George A. & Eather S. (Boots) Elliott
James W. (Jack) Jacobs
Rosella and Ed Raker of High Point
Louise and John Lawn of Magothy Beach
Marie F. Phelps
Roland & Catherine Geary
Thomas W. Tracey Sr. 12-28-34 10-9-94
Richard (Dick) Shoemaker
Katherine M. Tracey (1896-1999)
Mary Etta Jenkins Appleton 1894-1975
Oliver "BAMA" Goins
James W. Anderson
Carl B. Giles—loving husband & father
The Burton Family
Charlie & Jean Koontz
Preston Blake
May & John Wilson Sr.
Nick Liberatore
Ruth & William Upton Sr.
Thomas Edward Redmond
William L. Gable Sr.
Jean Holmes
Elmer & Gladys Grim

"Sunset on Stony Creek"
Photo: Blue Moon Aerial Photography

Sources

BOOKS

Burgess, Robert H. *This Was Chesapeake Bay*. Cambridge, MD: Cornell Maritime Press, 1963.

Burgess, Robert H. and H. Graham Wood. *Steamboats Out of Baltimore*. Cambridge, MD: Tidewater Publishers, 1968.

DAR Patriot Index. Washington: National Society of the American Revolution, 1966.

Gillespie, C. Richard. *The James Adams Floating Theatre*. Centreville, MD: Tidewater Publishers, 1991.

Hartzler, Daniel D. *Marylanders in the Confederacy*. Silver Spring, MD: Family Line, 1986.

Holland, F. Ross. *Maryland Lighthouses of the Chesapeake Bay*. Crownsville, MD: Maryland Historical Trust Press, and Colton's Point, MD: The Friends of St. Clement's Island Museum, 1977.

Keith, Robert C. *Baltimore Harbor: A Picture History*. Baltimore: Johns Hopkins University Press, 1991.

Kelly, Jacques. *Anne Arundel County: A Pictorial History*. Norfolk: The Donning Company, 1989.

Marine, William H. *The British Invasion of Maryland, 1812-1815*. Baltimore: Society of the War of 1812 in Maryland, 1913.

Nelker, Gladys. *Town Neck Hundred of Anne Arundel County*. Westminster, MD: Family Line Publication, 1990

Riley, Elihu S. *A History of Anne Arundel County in Maryland*. Annapolis: Charles G. Feldmeyer, 1905.

Smith, Captain John. *The Generall Historie of Virginia, New England, and the Summer Isles*. Volume I, Second and Third Books. Richmond: Franklin Press, 1819.

Taylor, Marianne. *My River Speaks: The History and Lore of the Magothy River*. Arnold, MD: Bay Media, Inc., 1998.

Travers, Paul J. *The Patapsco: Baltimore's River of History*. Centreville, MD: Tidewater Publishing Company, 1990.

Warfield, Joshua Dorsey. *The Founders of Anne Arundel and Howard Counties, Maryland*. Baltimore: Kohn and Pollock, 1905.

Wright, F. Edward. *Maryland Militia: War of 1812*. Vol. 4, Anne Arundel and Calvert Counties. Silver Spring, MD: Family Line, 1981.

ARTICLES

Bayside Beach News, Liz and Dennis Grimes, editors. "Marina Controversy." Issue 2 (Summer 1997):4; "Fatal Fire on Ship." Issue 4 (May 1998):5-6 .

Benson, Robert Louis. "Historical Survey of the Natural Resources of Anne Arundel County." *Anne Arundel County History Notes* 23, no.1 (October 1991): 11-13.

Blaisdell, Gail R. "Bloomer Girls Have Vanished." *Maryland Living*, July 7, 1968:4.

Cole, Merle T. "Fort Smallwood's Military Mission." *Anne Arundel County History Notes* 25, no. 3 (April 1994):1,6-7,9-10.

Cole, Merle T. "Army Air Defense Installations in Anne Arundel County, 1950-1973." *Anne Arundel County History Notes* 15, no.1 (Oct. 1983): 5-6.

Cunningham, Isabel S. "Anne Arundel's Famous Green-Meat Cantaloupes." *Anne Arundel County History Notes* 27, no.4 (July 1996): 3,4,8-10.

Durner, Marie Angel. "Early Days on Mountain Road." *Anne Arundel County History Notes* 16, no.3 (April 1985): 1-2.

Gould, Robert F. "Eminent Chemists of Maryland." *Maryland Historical Magazine* 80, no.1. (1985):19.

Kelbaugh, Jack. "By Water, Road, and Rail: The Early Railroads of Northern Anne Arundel County." *Anne Arundel County History Notes*, Part III, 23, no.3 (April 1992): 1,6,10-13; Part IV 23, no.4 (July 1992): 2,7,9-11.

McWilliams, Jane. "Land and People." *Anne Arundel County, Maryland: A Bicentennial History, 1649-1977*, edited by James C. Bradford. Annapolis: Anne Arundel County and Annapolis Bicentennial Committee, 1977: 1-10.

Mellin, Jack. "Green Haven Advertising Brochures." *Anne Arundel History Notes* 23, No.2 (Jan. 1991): 9 and no.3 (April 1991): 9-10.

Potee, Blodwin Shipley. "Bugeyes Docks, and Wharves." *Anne Arundel County History Notes* 16, no.2 (Jan. 1985): 1.

Potee, Blodwin Shipley. "The Squire's Tin House." *Anne Arundel County History Notes* 6, no.3 (April 1975): 1.

Robinson, John M. "The History of Pinehurst." *Anne Arundel County History Notes*, Part II 21, no.4 (July 1990): 1-2,7-8.

Slanker, Harold E., Jr. "The J.F. Johnson Lumber Company." *Anne Arundel County History Notes* XXIV, no.4 (July 1992): 2.

Stearnes, Richard E. "Indian Village Sites on the Magothy River, Anne Arundel County, Maryland." *Bulletin of the Natural History Society of Maryland* 8, no.3 (Nov. 1937): 15-19.

White, Roger B. "All Ashore for Fairview Park." *Anne Arundel County History Notes* 12, no.2 (Jan. 1981): 1-2.

White, Roger B. "Bus Service to Anne Arundel County: 1910-1980." *Anne Arundel County History Notes* 11, no.3 (April 1980): 1-3.

White, Roger B. "Saturday Night at the Dance Halls." *Anne Arundel County History Notes*, Part I, 20, no.4 (July 1989); Part II, 21, no.1 (October 1989): 1-6.

NEWSPAPERS

Evening Capital, Annapolis, 1884-1890.

Maryland Gazette, Annapolis, 1941-1993.

Maryland Republican, Annapolis, 1871, 1878.

The Sun, Baltimore, 1862-1999.

MAPS

Hopkins, G.M. Atlas of Anne Arundel County, Maryland, 1878. (Reprinted by the Greater Glen Burnie Jaycees, Glen Burnie, Maryland, 1969)

Martenet, Simon J. Map of Anne Arundel County, Maryland, 1860.

UNPUBLISHED MATERIAL

Anne Arundel County School Histories, 1952: Freetown, High Point, Jacobsville, Magothy, Pasadena, and Riviera Beach.

John A. Barnes. Letter to Henry A. Hancock. April 15, 1861.

Behm, Carl. "The Grachur Story: 1912-1992."

Hein, Bertha S. and Ruth E. Bollman. "A Church, Its People, Its Community." May, 1964. (Magothy Methodist Church and related history)

Kiessling, Trevor A., Jr. "Bodkin Neck: The Gateway to the Patapsco." 1979.

Kirkley, Charles F. "Report of the Committee to Study the Effects of Legalized Gambling in Anne Arundel County." May 1960.

McGrain, John W. "The Molinography of Anne Arundel County," no date.

Noue, Patricia. "Lake Waterford Park: Lake Waterford Dam Repair and Impact on the Environment." 1993.

Potee, Blodwin Shipley. "The History of Mt. Carmel Methodist Church, 1884-1979."

Pritchett, Virginia Aten. "A History of Magothy Methodist Church, 1777-1977." (Revised by Helen Coggins)

Schramm, Emma M. "History of the Pasadena Post Office and All Other Post Offices That Covered This Same Area." November 1985.

Schramm, Emma M. "Sixty Years in Anne Arundel County: The Schramm Farm, 1910-1970."

Ware, Donna M. "A Self-Guiding Brochure for Hancock's Resolution."

Zambala, Dennis. Maryland Historical Trust Historic Sites Inventory for Seven-Foot Knoll Lighthouse. Survey No. AA-931, August 5, 1987.

Vertical files at the Maryland Historical Society, Anne Arundel County Historical Society's Kuethe Library, Riviera Beach Library, and Mountain Road Library.

RECORDS

Act of Maryland State Legislature Relating to Public Roads in Anne Arundel County, Jan. 3, 1800. (Liber J.G., No.3, f.350)

Agricultural Census, Anne Arundel County, 1850 (Microfilm 5164-1, State Archives)

Archives of Maryland, Oaths of Fidelity, 1777-1781. (Red Book 22:27, 27.1)

Census, Anne Arundel County, Maryland, 1850. Pasadena, MD:Anne Arundel County Genealogical Society, 1991. Compiled by John W. Powell.

Census, Book #3, Third and Fifth Districts, Anne Arundel County, 1860. (130-157, Johnson's Store)

Civil War Enrollment Records, Anne Arundel County, Third District, 1862.

Federal Direct Tax, 1798. Maryland State Papers.

Heads of Families at the First Census of the United States Taken in the Year 1890: Maryland. Washington, Government Printing Office, 1907.

Muster Rolls and Other Records of Maryland Troops in the American Revolution, Archives of Maryland, Vol.XVIII. Baltimore: Maryland Historical Society, 1900.

Slave Census, Anne Arundel County, 1960 (Microfilm 7202, Maryland State Archives)

Index

Mr. George W. Calvert

Baltimore, Md. _____ 1901.

C. A. ROBINS___

Bought of C. N. ROBINSON & BRO.
..DEALERS IN..
FARMERS' SUPPLIES,
507 E. PRATT STREET

Garden Seeds,
Peas, Small Fruit
and
Vegetable Plants,
Fertilizers.

Boss Plows,
Agricultural Implements,
Peach and Strawberry
Crates and Baskets.

1901   Terms:

July 20	To Amount brought forward			5368 2
	" 1 bag millet b bag		1 00	
20	" 1 bag of meal b bag		1 40	
	" 25 lbs of paris green	@ .05	1 25	
	" 1 bag for millet	" .10½	2 63	64
July 18	By 29 bags ret'd		15	
Aug 15	" 2 coal oil bbls ret'd	@ .15	1 00	
July 26	3 bu Turnip seed	" .80	05	

ARMIGER 119-R

O. A. FUSS
ONE-STOP SERVICE

MOUNTAIN RD. & ANNAPOLIS BLVD., MILLERSVILLE, MD.

TO Schramm Bros.   Pasadena Md   DATE 10/9/4_

Gravel

8 Esso   1.56
2.34

9/26

10/

RADIO SERVICE
FT. SMALLWOOD RD.
BALTIMORE 26, MD.
CLinton 5-5200

Date 4/23/70

Miss Schramm

| DESCRIPTION | | | | | AMOUNT |
| AM-FM-PS-A__ | | | | | 69 90 |

ARMIGER 707

BROOKS FARM EQUIPMENT
Ritchie Highway at Elvaton
PASADENA, MARYLAND

SALES   CASE   SERVICE

24 DISK 18"   243 64

KLUG BROTHERS
ESSO SERVICENTER
Mountain & Mill Roads, Pasadena, Md.
Atlas Tires, Batteries & Accessories
ARMIGER 500

12-9-55   19

Name Schramm

Address